Fiesta Mexicana

by

Toby Arias

and

Elaine Frassanito

Cover design and drawings by Judy Elder

Fifth Printing, 1990

ISBN 0-9609942-0-3

Copyright ©1982 by T & E Enterprises

CONTENTS

	Page
Introduction	
Glossary	i
Basic Techniques and Sauces	1
Appetizers	5
Beverages	20
Breads, Soups, and Salads	23
Main Dishes	36
Egg Dishes	68
Vegetables	73
Desserts	81
Index	88

INTRODUCTION

Our love for Mexican food with a distinctive New Mexican accent has inspired us to write this book. It is a collection of favorite recipes from the kitchens of friends whose culinary talents have created the most delectable and exciting dishes in the Southwest.

As transplanted Easterners, we are intrigued by the intermingling of cultures in New Mexico and have attempted to combine the exotic tastes and flavors of the old world with new world innovations.

Concisely written, with easy-to-follow instructions, Fiesta Mexicana is a must for both the experienced and novice cook. We hope the addition of our recipes will lend zest and originality to your family menu.

GLOSSARY

albondigas	meatballs
arroz	rice
arroz con pollo	rice with chicken
biscochitos	anise-flavored cookies
buñuelos	a fried bread round sprinkled with cinnamon and sugar
burritos	rolled flour tortillas with a variety of fillings
calabacitas	squash
caldillo	stew
capirotada (sopa)	bread pudding
carne adovada	pork marinated in red chili sauce
carne asada	grilled marinated steak
chalupas	"little boats"; corn tortilla cups with a variety of fillings
chili con queso	melted cheese and green chili
chili (green)	a long green pepper, used as a basic seasoning in Mexican food
chili (red)	a green chili allowed to ripen, usually dried and used as a basic seasoning in Mexican food
chili rellenos	a green chili, stuffed with cheese, dipped in batter and deep fried
chimichanga	a stuffed flour tortilla, deep fried
chorizo	spicy Mexican sausage

cilantro	fresh coriander, a common spice
cumin (comino)	a common Mexican spice
empañadas	turnover, stuffed with meat or fruit
enchiladas	flat or rolled corn tortillas, covered with red or green chili sauce, meat, and cheese
fajita	marinated meat or poultry
flan	custard
flautas (flute)	a variety of taco
frijoles	beans
frijoles refritos	refried beans
garbanzos	chick peas
gazpacho	a cold vegetable soup
guacamole	avocado salad and dip
huevos	eggs
Indian fry bread	deep-fried bread round, usually served with honey
jalapeños	small, green, extra hot chili
masa	corn meal used to make tortillas and tamales
masa harina	commercially prepared corn meal
molletes	anise-flavored bun
nachos	tortilla chips covered with melted cheese
natillas	custard pudding
pollo	chicken

iii

picadillo	meat and almond stew, also used as a dip
posole	hominy and pork stew, garnished with red chili
pastelitos	pastry crust filled with dried fruit
quesadilla	a deep-fried corn tortilla, stuffed with cheese
quelites	spinach with pinto beans
refried beans	cooked pinto beans, mashed and fried in bacon fat
ristra	a string of red chilies
salsa	sauce
sopa (capirotada)	bread pudding
sopaipillas	puffy, deep-fried "pillow" of dough, traditionally served with honey
taco	a folded corn tortilla, fried crisp and stuffed with a variety of meat, cheese, beans, and garnishes
tamale	shredded pork in red chili, encased in masa wrapped in a cornhusk and steamed
taquitas	rolled tacos, deep fat fried
tostadas compuestas	a crisp corn tortilla cup, stuffed with a variety of fillings
tostados	crisp corn tortilla chips
tortillas	a flat bread made of white flour or corn flour

BASIC TECHNIQUES AND SAUCES

CHILI

Chili is a unique and flavorful ingredient, basic to all Mexican cooking. Green chili turns to red at an advanced stage of maturity, and both yield their own distinctive taste. Most of the "heat" in chili is found in the seeds and veins. Be sure to remove these seeds and veins during preparation. Remember that green chilies must always be peeled for use in recipes, whereas red chilies are processed with skins.

Red and green chilies are easily prepared according to the following directions. They are also available canned, frozen, and dried throughout the country. Although the use of fresh chili is preferable, our recipes generally call for canned chili because it is more readily available in most areas.

PREPARATION OF FRESH GREEN CHILI

Rinse and drain chilies. Using a fork or toothpick, perforate outer skin to permit steam to escape. Place chilies directly on a hot grill or in broiler and roast until chilies are uniformly blistered (turn frequently to prevent burning). Remove chilies from broiler or grill and place in a bowl or on a cookie sheet. Cover chilies with a cold, damp dishtowel for 5 minutes. Starting at stem end, peel the outer skin downward. Remove the stem and seeds. The chili is now ready to use in any recipe. To freeze green chilies, leave skins on and store in plastic bags. Peel after thawing.

GREEN CHILI SAUCE
(yields 2 cups)

    2 tablespoons vegetable oil
    1 clove garlic
    2 tablespoons onion, minced
    1 tablespoon flour
    1 cup water
    1/4 teaspoon salt
    1 cup green chili, diced

Sauté garlic and onion in oil until tender. Blend in flour and stir until lightly browned. Add water, salt, and chili and simmer for 5 minutes. Serve on enchiladas (see index), hamburgers, and other recipes calling for green chili sauce.

BLENDER GREEN CHILI SAUCE
(yields 1-2 quarts)

    12-18 green chilies
    1/2 teaspoon salt
    1 teaspoon garlic salt
    1 teaspoon oregano
    water

Remove skins and seeds from fresh roasted chilies. Fill blender 1/2 full with chilies. Cover with water; add salt, garlic salt, and oregano and process on low speed. Add more water and chilies as necessary until the consistency is that of a heavy tomato sauce. Repeat the blender process until all the chilies are used. Simmer sauce on low heat for 30 minutes. Use immediately for green chili enchiladas (see index) or allow to cool, pour into 8-ounce containers (margarine tubs are handy to use), and freeze until needed.

PREPARATION OF DRIED RED CHILIES
(yields 1-2 quarts)

>18-24 dried red chili pods
>2 cloves garlic
>water
>salt to taste
>dash of oregano (optional)

Soak red chili pods about 15 minutes in warm water to soften. Open each pod and rinse thoroughly under running warm water. Remove stems, blemishes, and seeds. The heat of chili is in the veins and seeds: for hotter chili, leave veins; for milder chili, remove veins. Fill an electric blender about 1/2 full of red chili pods. Cover with water no more than 2 inches from the top. Add garlic. Blend for several minutes until smooth and skins are completely blended. Add additional water if necessary to make a smooth consistency. Add salt to taste. Repeat process until chili pods are all blended. Simmer sauce for about 15 minutes. Sauce may be poured into containers and frozen until needed. Serve on enchiladas; use in tamales, carne adovada, etc. (see index).

RED CHILI POWDER
(yields 1 cup)

>16 dried red chili pods

Place 3 or 4 chilies in blender and process on low until completely powdered. Repeat process until all the pods are used. Store in jar in refrigerator or freezer.

POWDERED RED CHILI SAUCE
(yields 1 quart)

    1/4 cup lard or shortening
    1/4 cup flour
    1/4 cup red chili powder
    2 cups beef stock or water
    1/2 teaspoon salt
    1/4 teaspoon garlic powder

Melt lard or shortening and slowly add flour, blending well. Cook slowly, stirring until flour is just lightly browned, about 5 minutes. Add the chili powder and stir until moistened. Slowly add beef stock or water and blend well so no lumps remain. Add salt and garlic powder and simmer for about 10 minutes. Use in any recipe calling for red chili sauce.

PREPARATION OF FRESH RED CHILI
(yields 1-2 quarts)

    18-24 fresh red chili pods
    1/4 teaspoon oregano
    2 cloves garlic
    2 teaspoons salt

Wash chilies and remove stems. Slit each chili open with knife and, under running water, remove seeds and veins. The "heat" in chilies is in the seeds and veins: for hotter chili, allow some veins to remain; for milder chili, remove all seeds and veins. Place chilies on cookie sheet and bake at 250° for about 10 minutes. Remove from oven, cover with towel, and let "steam" for 5 minutes. Fill blender 1/2 full with chilies, add 1 cup water, and blend on low. Add oregano, garlic, salt, and more water as necessary for a good "sauce" consistency. Continue to add chilies and water until blender is full but not overflowing. Continue processing chilies until all are blended. Simmer sauce for 15 minutes. Use in any recipe calling for red chili sauce.

APPETIZERS

TORTILLA CHIPS (TOSTADOS)
(yields 96 chips)

While packaged tortilla chips can be readily purchased throughout the country, freshly fried chips are a taste treat and so simple to make.

    1 dozen corn tortillas
    vegetable oil
    salt

With kitchen shears, cut each tortilla into 8 pie-shaped wedges, leaving them attached in the center. Fry each round in 1/2 inch of very hot oil until crisp, turning once. Drain on paper towels and sprinkle with salt. Poke the center of each tortilla and it will separate into 8 even chips. Serve with dips or salsa (see index).

PICANTE SAUCE
(yields 6 quarts)

    24 large tomatoes
    3 green chilies
    3 red chilies
    6 onions
    4 hot peppers
    4 tablespoons salt
    1-1/3 cups vinegar
    celery salt to taste
    mustard seed to taste

Simmer all ingredients for 2-3 hours. Allow to cool, pour into freezer containers, and defrost as needed.

TACO SAUCE WITH JALAPEÑOS
(yields 2 cups)

    2 cups whole peeled tomatoes
    5-6 fresh jalapeño peppers
    2 small cloves of garlic
    salt to taste

Pull stems off jalapeños and put all ingredients in a blender for 10 to 15 seconds. May be served as a dip.

GREEN CHILI SALSA
(yields 1 pint)

    2 large tomatoes, finely chopped
    1 Bermuda onion, minced
    3/4 teaspoon garlic salt
    4 green chilies, chopped

Combine tomatoes and onion. Stir in garlic salt and chilies, blending well. Serve as a dip with tortilla chips or wherever salsa is called for.

BROCCOLI DIP
(yields 5 cups)

    1 10-ounce package frozen chopped broccoli
    2 cans condensed cream of chicken soup
    1/4 teaspoon garlic
    3 cups monterey jack cheese, grated
    2 4-ounce cans green chili, chopped

Cook broccoli according to package directions. Drain well. Add remaining ingredients to broccoli and heat until cheese melts. Serve with tostados.

ALBUQUERQUE DELIGHT
(serves 12)

    1 can refried beans (with onion and green chili if available)
    1 package taco seasoning mix
    3 avocados, mashed (or 1 package frozen avocado mix)
    2 teaspoons lemon juice
    2 tablespoons onion, minced
    dash of garlic salt
    4 ounces sour cream
    1 cup green chili, chopped
    1/2 pound monterey jack cheese, grated
    1/2 pound longhorn cheddar cheese, grated
    2 ripe tomatoes, chopped
    1 can pitted black olives, sliced for garnish

Blend refried beans with taco mix. Spread into large pie dish. To mashed avocados, add lemon juice, onions, and garlic salt (omit if using frozen avocado mix). Spread avocado mixture over bean layer. Add layers of sour cream, green chili, and cheeses. Garnish with tomatoes and olives and serve with tortilla chips.

GREEN CHILI DIP
(yields 3 cups)

    1/2 pound sharp cheddar cheese
    1/2 pound monterey jack cheese
    1 medium onion, grated
    1 teaspoon garlic powder
    1 teaspoon oregano
    1/2 teaspoon cumin
    2 ripe medium tomatoes, finely chopped
    1/2 cup evaporated milk
    2 4-ounce cans green chili, chopped

Melt cheeses in top of double boiler. Add remaining ingredients and heat, blending well. Serve with tortilla chips.

CHILI CON QUESO
(serves 15 to 20)

    1 pound velveeta cheese
    6 green chilies, chopped
    1 jalapeño pepper, chopped (optional)
    1/4 cup onion, chopped
    3 tomatoes, finely chopped
    dash of garlic salt

Melt cheese in top of double boiler. Add rest of ingredients and simmer for 5 minutes, stirring often to avoid burning. Serve warm with tortilla chips.

EASY CHILI CON QUESO
(serves 15 to 20)

    1 pound velveeta cheese, cubed
    1/4 cup milk
    1 small jar picante sauce

Melt cheese in milk in top of double boiler. Add 2 tablespoons picante sauce. Taste. Add more sauce as needed for desired "hotness". Serve with tortilla chips.

JALAPEÑO BEAN DIP
(serves 12)

    1/2 cup onion, minced
    1 tablespoon butter
    2 cups refried beans
    1/2 pound monterey jack cheese, cubed
    1 4-ounce can green chili, chopped

Sauté onion in butter. In top of double boiler, combine all ingredients and heat thoroughly. Serve in chafing dish with tortilla chips.

PICADILLO ALMOND DIP
(yields 6 cups)

    1/2 pound ground beef
    1/2 pound ground pork
    1 teaspoon salt
    1/4 teaspoon pepper
    4 medium tomatoes, peeled and diced
    2 cloves garlic, minced
    3 green onions, minced
    1 6-ounce can tomato paste
    2 jalapeño peppers, rinsed, seeded, and diced
    dash of oregano
    3/4 cup pimento, chopped
    3/4 cup seedless raisins
    3/4 cup whole, blanched almonds

Combine pork and beef in heavy saucepan and brown. Add salt and pepper. Cover meat with water. Bring to a boil, reduce heat, and simmer for 30 minutes. Drain off excess liquid and add remaining ingredients. Return to boiling; reduce heat and simmer for 45 minutes or until mixture is very thick. Serve hot with tortilla chips.

GUACAMOLE
(serves 4)

    2 ripe avocados, peeled and mashed
    1-1/2 tablespoons lemon juice
    1 small ripe tomato, chopped
    2 tablespoons onion, finely chopped
    1/2 teaspoon salt
    1/2 teaspoon garlic powder
    2 tablespoons green chili, finely chopped
      (optional)

To mashed avocados, add remaining ingredients. Blend well. Serve chilled with tortilla chips.

SOUR CREAM-CHILI DIP
(serves 6)

    1 cup sour cream
    1 4-ounce can green chili, chopped
    1/2 teaspoon garlic salt

Combine all ingredients. Chill to blend flavors and serve with tortilla chips.

CHILI TEMPURA
(serves 6-8)

    1-1/2 pounds cooked chicken, cubed
    8 green chilies, peeled and sliced lengthwise
      into 1/2 inch slices
    4 cups vegetable oil
    1-1/2 cups pancake batter

Wrap green chili around chicken cubes and secure with toothpick. Refrigerate. Heat oil in deep fryer to about 350° or until a cube of bread browns in 40-60 seconds. Prepare pancake batter and beat until smooth. Roll chili/chicken bits in batter and fry in hot oil until browned. Drain and serve as is or with chili con queso.

CHILI EGG ROLLS
(serves 24)

    2 pounds ground beef
    1 onion, finely chopped
    1/4 teaspoon garlic powder
    1 teaspoon salt
    1 teaspoon ground cumin
    1 8-ounce can green chili, drained and chopped
    4 cups longhorn cheddar cheese, grated
    24 egg roll skins
    2 egg whites, beaten

Brown beef and drain well. Add onion, seasonings, and chili. Cook until onions are soft. Remove from heat, add cheese, and mix well. Place about 2 tablespoons of meat mixture just below the center of each egg roll skin. Bring sides in 1/4 inch, and fold from bottom up until rolled. Seal edge with whipped egg white. Deep fry at 325° until golden brown. Drain and cut into thirds. Serve hot.

GREEN CHILI WON TONS
(yields 40)

    1 pound longhorn cheddar cheese, grated
    1 8-ounce can green chili, chopped
    2 packages won ton skins
    oil

Combine cheese and green chilies. Place 1 teaspoon of mixture on a won ton skin and fold like an envelope. Fry in 2 inches of hot oil, turning once until golden brown. Drain.

TOSSED SHRIMP
(serves 6)

    3 dozen small cooked shrimp, peeled and deveined
    1/2 cup lime juice
    2 medium tomatoes, chopped
    1 small onion, finely chopped
    1 large avocado, peeled and cubed
    1 4-ounce can green chili, chopped
    2 tablespoons coriander leaves, finely chopped
    3 tablespoons vegetable oil
    salt and pepper to taste

Toss shrimp lightly with rest of ingredients. Serve cold with flour tortilla wedges. Tastes best if served within one hour of preparation.

ALBONDIGAS
(serves 10)

Meatballs

    2 pounds ground beef
    1 cup bread crumbs
    1/4 cup onion, finely chopped
    2 teaspoons salt
    1 teaspoon pepper
    1/8 teaspoon garlic powder
    1-1/2 teaspoons ground coriander seed
    1/2 cup flour

Sauce

    6 tablespoons corn oil
    6 cups hot water
    1 tablespoon ground coriander seed
    salt to taste
    2 cloves garlic
    5 medium potatoes (optional)

ALBONDIGAS (continued)

Combine meatball ingredients and mix well. For appetizers, shape into small balls; for main dishes, larger balls. Roll balls in flour, coating lightly. Heat oil and fry meatballs until browned. Add water, coriander, salt, garlic (and potatoes for main dish). Simmer for 30 minutes (or until potatoes are tender).

FONDUE MEXICANA
(serves 8)

    12 ounces longhorn cheddar cheese, grated
    1 medium onion, finely chopped
    1 4-ounce can green chili, chopped
    8 slices bacon, cooked and crumbled

Combine all ingredients except bacon in a fondue pot. Heat until cheese is melted, stirring frequently. Add bacon. Keep warm over low heat. Serve with tortilla chips.

SPICY CASHEWS
(serves 8)

    2 cups cashew nuts
    1-1/2 tablespoons butter
    1 teaspoon salt
    1/4 teaspoon powdered red chili
    1/2 teaspoon ground cumin
    1/2 teaspoon ground coriander

Sauté nuts in butter about 10 minutes. Remove and drain well on paper towels. Place nuts, salt, chili, and spices in a paper bag and shake well until nuts are well coated.

CHILI-CHEESE LOG

    2 8-ounce packages cream cheese, softened
    1 pound pasteurized process American cheese, grated
    1/3 cup green chili, chopped
    1 teaspoon garlic powder
    red chili powder
    parsley
    1-1/2 cups pecans, finely chopped

Combine cheeses, chili, and garlic powder and mix well. Chill until firm enough to be handled. Form mixture into 2 log shapes by rolling between waxed paper. Roll in red chili, parsley, and nuts to coat. Refrigerate 4-6 hours, slice, and serve on your favorite crackers.

CHILI-CHEESE BALLS
(serves 6)

    1/2 pound sharp cheddar cheese, grated
    1/2 cup margarine, softened
    1 cup flour
    1/2 teaspoon salt
    1 4-ounce can green chili, chopped

Combine all ingredients and mix well. Form dough into 3/4-inch balls. Bake at 375° for 12-15 minutes. Can be frozen and then baked about 18 minutes.

CHILI-PECAN BALLS
(serves 8-10)

    1 8-ounce package cream cheese, softened
    3/4 pound sharp cheddar cheese, grated
    2 8-ounce cans green chili, chopped and drained
    1 cup pecans, finely chopped

CHILI-PECAN BALLS (continued)

Combine cheeses. Stir in green chili and mix well. Form into bite-sized balls and roll in pecans. Chill until firm. Serve with crackers.

CHEESE CRISP
(serves 1)

    1 large flour tortilla
    3/4 cup monterey jack or cheddar cheese, grated
    2 tablespoons salsa (see index) or use canned salsa

Preheat broiler. Place tortilla on an ungreased cookie sheet. Sprinkle generously with grated cheese. Top with salsa. Broil until cheese bubbles. Slice with pizza cutter and serve immediately.

CHEESE CRISP WITH GUACAMOLE
(serves 12)

    1 dozen flour tortillas
    butter
    2 pounds sharp cheddar cheese
    12 green chilies, chopped
    2 cups guacamole (optional - see index)

Place tortillas on an ungreased baking sheet. Spread lightly with butter on one side of tortilla. Cover tortilla with cheddar cheese to within 1/4 inch of outer edge. Sprinkle each tortilla with green chili. Broil until edges of tortilla are slightly browned and cheese has melted. Top with guacamole. Cut with pizza cutter and serve hot.

CHEESE QUICHE
(serves 4-6)

      1 9-inch pie crust
      1 cup cheddar cheese, grated
      1 cup monterey jack cheese, grated
      3 large eggs
      1 teaspoon salt
      1/4 teaspoon pepper
      1-1/2 cups half and half
      1 4-ounce can green chili, chopped
      1 can ripe black olives, sliced
      2 tablespoons green onion, finely chopped

Preheat oven to 350°. Mix the cheeses together and spread on bottom of the pie crust. In a bowl, combine remaining ingredients. Pour egg mixture over cheese-covered pie shell. Bake for 45 minutes or until a knife inserted comes out clean.

CHILI PIE
(serves 6-8)

      8 whole green chilies, peeled and seeded
      1/4 pound cheddar cheese, grated
      5 eggs, slightly beaten
      2 tablespoons cream or milk
      3/4 teaspoon salt
      fresh ground black pepper

Cut chilies open and line greased 10-inch pie pan or casserole, allowing chilies to come to top edge of pan. Blend remaining ingredients. Pour over chilies and bake at 350° for 30 minutes or until set. Serve in bite-sized pieces for appetizer or in wedges as an accompaniment.

NACHOS
(yields 4 dozen)

    48 tortilla chips
    12 ounces monterey jack or cheddar cheese, grated
    4 jalapeño peppers, diced

Top each chip with a mound of cheese and piece of jalapeño. On cookie sheet, broil slightly until cheese melts. May also be cooked in dish in microwave about 1 minute or until cheese melts. Serve hot.

Variations: Sour cream, chili con queso, chopped tomatoes, and refried beans may be added to each chip. Green chili may be used instead of jalapeños.

QUESADILLAS
(serves 12)

    1 dozen corn tortillas
    oil
    1 pound monterey jack or longhorn cheddar cheese, grated
    8-10 green chilies, chopped
    avocado (optional)
    tomato (optional)
    sour cream (optional)

Lightly fry tortillas in 1/8 inch hot oil just until softened (about 30 seconds). Drain on paper towels. Combine cheese and chili and place a heaping tablespoon of the mixture on each tortilla. Roll and fry quickly in 1 inch of hot oil until crisp, turning once, about 1 minute. Top with sliced avocado, tomato, and/or sour cream if desired.

CHILI-CHEESE STICKS
(serves 12)

    3 tablespoons green chili, chopped
    3/4 cup flour
    1/2 teaspoon salt
    1/4 cup shortening
    1/3 cup longhorn cheddar cheese, grated
    1 egg white, slightly beaten

Drain chili and reserve liquid. Sift flour and salt and cut in shortening. Stir in chili and cheese. Sprinkle with reserved chili liquid, adding water if necessary to make mixture moist enough to be pressed into a ball. Roll out dough to 1/4-1/8 inch thick. Cut into 1/2 x 4 inch strips. Brush with egg white. Bake on lightly greased cookie sheet at 425° about 10 minutes or until golden brown. Serve hot or cold.

CHILI-STUFFED MUSHROOMS
(serves 20)

    70 large mushrooms
    2-1/2 sticks butter or margarine
    3 cloves garlic
    3 small green onions, chopped
    2 4-ounce cans green chili, chopped
    1/2 cup fine bread crumbs
    1/2 teaspoon salt
    1/4 teaspoon pepper
    1/8 teaspoon dry mustard
    1/2 teaspoon nutmeg
    2 tablespoons grated parmesan cheese

Wash mushrooms. Remove stems and chop. Cook garlic in butter 1 minute. Dip mushroom caps in butter until coated and place on cookie sheet. Reheat butter remaining in skillet and sauté onions and mushroom stems until soft (about 10 minutes). Add the chili, bread crumbs, seasonings, and cheese and mix well. Mound mixture into mushroom caps. Bake uncovered at 375° for 15 minutes. May be frozen and reheated in oven or microwave.

HOT CARNE ADOVADA CANAPES
(serves 8)

    1 pound lean pork, sliced thin
    3 cups thick red chili sauce
    1/4 teaspoon oregano
    1 clove garlic
    flour tortillas

Combine all ingredients and marinate in refrigerator about 24 hours, turning meat so it is evenly covered. Bake at 325° for 1-1/2 to 2 hours or until pork is tender. Serve hot on flour tortilla wedge.

BISCUIT PIZZA
(yields 40)

    1 pound ground beef
    1 tube refrigerator biscuits
    1 7-1/2 ounce can Spanish-style tomato sauce
    2 4-ounce cans green chili, chopped
    1/2 pound mozzarella cheese, grated

Brown beef and drain well. Divide biscuits and form into 10 flat circles on cookie sheet. Spread each with tomato sauce. Add a layer of meat, then chili, and top with mozzarella. Bake at 300° for 15-20 minutes. Cut into quarters and serve hot.

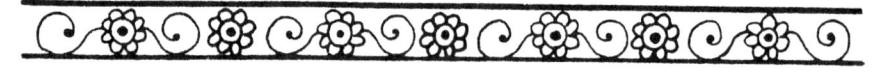

BEVERAGES

SPICED TEA
(serves 30)

    2 cups Tang
    1 package instant lemonade
    1 to 1-1/2 cups instant ice tea mix
    2-1/2 cups sugar
    2 teaspoons cinnamon
    1 teaspoon ground cloves

Combine all ingredients and use 2 teaspoons per cup of boiling water. Store in jars and use as needed.

CAFE KAHLÚA
(serves 4)

    4 cups hot brewed coffee
    4 ounces Kahlúa
    2 ounces brandy
    4 teaspoons chocolate syrup
    dash ground cinnamon
    whipped cream

Blend liqueurs, syrup, and cinnamon. Stir in hot coffee. Pour into 4 serving cups and top each with whipped cream.

CAFE MEXICANA
(serves 4)

>32 ounces hot brewed coffee
>4 ounces rum
>4 ounces Kahlúa
>4 teaspoons brown sugar
>whipped cream
>4 1-inch sticks of cinnamon

Blend coffee with liqueurs and brown sugar. Place 1 cinnamon stick into bottom of each of 4 cups. Pour hot coffee mixture into each cup and top each with 3 tablespoons whipped cream.

SPANISH COFFEE
(serves 4)

>4 cups hot brewed coffee
>4 teaspoons sugar
>6 ounces Kahlúa
>whipped cream
>chocolate shavings

Stir sugar into hot coffee. Add Kahlúa. Pour into 4 serving cups. Top each with dollop of whipped cream and sprinkle with chocolate shavings.

BEBIDO DE STRAWBERRY
(serves 4)

>1-1/2 pints strawberries
>3 cups cold milk
>2 tablespoons sugar
>mint leaves

Clean and hull strawberries. Place all ingredients in blender and puree until drink is frothy. Pour into 4 tall glasses and garnish with mint leaves.

NEW MEXICAN HOT CHOCOLATE
(serves 4)

    3 ounces semisweet chocolate
    2 tablespoons sugar
    1/2 teaspoon cinnamon
    1/4 teaspoon vanilla extract
    3 cups milk
    whipped cream (optional)

Place all ingredients in saucepan. Bring to boil, stirring constantly until chocolate melts. Beat with rotary beater until well blended. Mixture may be frothy. Pour into 4 individual cups. Top with whipped cream if desired.

MARGARITAS
(serves 2)

    3 ounces tequila
    1 ounce triple sec
    2 ounces lime juice
    coarsely ground salt

Moisten rims of stem cocktail glasses with lime wedge. Dip rims in salt (table salt may be used). Shake rest of ingredients with cracked ice. Strain into glasses and sip over the salted edge.

BREADS, SOUPS, SALADS

FLOUR TORTILLAS
(yields 12)

    4 cups flour
    1-1/2 teaspoons salt
    2 teaspoons baking powder
    4 tablespoons shortening
    2 cups warm water

In mixing bowl, combine flour, salt, and baking powder. Cut in shortening. Add warm water, a small amount at a time, and use hands to form dough. Add water only as necessary. Knead dough until it is smooth. Cover and let stand for 10-15 minutes. Divide dough into egg-sized balls. On floured surface, roll out each ball into a 6-inch circle, about 1/8 inch thick. Try to keep them as round as possible. Cook each round on hot, ungreased griddle about 2 minutes on each side or until speckled. Cover to keep warm and soft until served. To freeze, allow to cool, wrap well, and store until needed. These are a real taste treat!

CORN TORTILLAS
(yields 12)

These corn tortillas are fairly easy to make, but the store-bought variety are equally tasty and so economical that we recommend the use of pre-packaged tortillas.

    2 cups corn masa harina
    1 teaspoon salt
    1-2/3 cups boiling water

Combine corn masa harina and salt. Add boiling water and stir until dough is the consistency of

CORN TORTILLAS (continued)

thick oatmeal. Set aside for 30 minutes. Wet hands slightly and form dough into 12 egg-sized balls. Between 2 pieces of waxed paper, roll dough out very thin, being careful to obtain a circle shape. Bake each on lightly greased, preheated skillet, turning once, until lightly browned on each side.

SOPAIPILLAS
(yields 4 dozen)

    4 cups flour
    2 teaspoons baking powder
    1 teaspoon salt
    4 tablespoons shortening
    3/4 cup warm water
    vegetable oil
    honey

Combine dry ingredients and cut in shortening. Add water and mix well, working dough until smooth. Cover and let stand 20 minutes. Preheat about 2 inches vegetable oil to 420°. Roll dough to 1/8-inch thickness on a lightly floured board. Cut into 3- or 4-inch squares and fry until golden on both sides, turning once. If the fat is sufficiently hot, the sopaipillas will puff and become hollow shortly after being dropped into it. Drain sopaipillas on paper towels. Serve warm with honey. These "little pillows" are traditional accompaniments with Mexican meals and can be served either as a bread or as a dessert.

INDIAN FRY BREAD
(yields 12)

    2 cups flour
    1/3 cup powdered milk
    2 teaspoons baking powder
    1 teaspoon salt
    2 tablespoons lard
    3/4 cup warm water
    oil

Mix dry ingredients. Cut in 1 tablespoon lard until crumbly. Add water and mix until a soft dough forms. Knead until dough is smooth and springy in texture. Divide into 12 balls. Melt 1 tablespoon of lard and brush onto each dough ball. Set aside for 30 minutes. On a lightly floured surface, roll ball to a 4-inch circle. Then stretch with hands to 7 or 8 inches in diameter. Poke hole in center. Fry in oil at 365° until lightly browned, turning once. Serve with butter or honey.

BUÑUELOS (FRIED BREAD)
(yields 6 dozen)

    3-1/2 cups sifted all-purpose flour
    1 teaspoon salt
    1 teaspoon baking powder
    1-1/2 teaspoons sugar
    1/4 cup butter, softened
    2 eggs
    1/2 cup milk
    vegetable oil
    1 cup sugar
    1 teaspoon cinnamon

Sift flour again with salt, baking powder, and sugar. Cut in butter until mixture resembles coarse meal. Beat eggs lightly with milk, then pour into flour mixture and stir until a solid mass forms. Knead dough lightly for 2 minutes or until smooth and elastic. Form dough into balls the size

BUÑUELOS (continued)

of a walnut and let stand 15 minutes. Preheat oil to 420°. Roll each ball on a lightly floured board into a very thin circle, about 4 inches in diameter. Cut a hole in center with a thimble. Place circles of dough in a single layer on waxed paper until all are rolled and ready for deep frying. Fry in hot, deep fat until puffed and golden brown, about 30 seconds on each side. Drain on paper towels. Mix sugar and cinnamon in a paper bag. Place buñuelos, one at a time, in the bag and shake gently until well coated with mixture.

MOLLETES
(yields 3 to 3-1/2 dozen)

    1 package active dry yeast
    2 tablespoons sugar
    2 cups warm water
    1/2 cup shortening
    1-1/2 cups sugar
    2 eggs
    1 teaspoon salt
    1 teaspoon anise seed
    6-7 cups flour
    butter

Dissolve yeast and sugar in warm water in large bowl. In a smaller bowl, cream shortening with sugar. Beat eggs in, one at a time. Add salt and anise seed. Add creamed mixture to yeast and thoroughly combine. Add flour gradually to make a moderately firm dough. Knead on a lightly floured board until smooth and elastic. Place in a greased bowl, cover, and allow to double in bulk again. Preheat oven to 375°. Knead dough and mold into round buns the size of an egg. Place in a well greased pan, cover, and allow to double in bulk. Brush lightly with butter and bake 20 to 25 minutes in a 375° oven.

MEXICAN SPOON BREAD

1-1/2 cups cornmeal
1 teaspoon salt
1 teaspoon baking powder
1/2 teaspoon baking soda
1/3 cup vegetable oil
1 pound cream-style corn
2 eggs beaten
8 ounces green chili, chopped
2 cups longhorn cheddar cheese, grated

Combine all ingredients except chili and cheese. Pour half of the batter into a greased 9 x 9 inch baking dish. Layer with half of green chilies and sprinkle with half of the cheese. Repeat layers and bake at 375° for 45 minutes until firm.

ZUCCHINI SOUP
(yields 6 cups)

4 medium zucchini, quartered and sliced
2 15-ounce cans chicken broth
1 onion, finely chopped
1-1/2 teaspoon salt
1/2 teaspoon pepper
dill weed to taste
1 4-ounce can green chili, chopped
2 8-ounce packages cream cheese
1 cup sour cream with chives
chopped chives for garnish

In a saucepan, add zucchini, chicken broth, onion, salt, pepper, dill weed, and chili. Simmer mixture until squash is soft (20-30 minutes). Blend the cream cheese and sour cream in a blender until smooth. Fold zucchini mixture a little at a time into cheese and sour cream and blend in blender. Chill overnight or until very cold. Garnish with chopped chives.

CREAM OF ZUCCHINI SOUP
(serves 6)

    2 tablespoons butter
    4 tablespoons onion, finely chopped
    3 cups unpeeled zucchini, diced
    4 cups chicken broth
    1 teaspoon dill weed
    1-1/2 cups plain yogurt
    salt and pepper to taste

Sauté onion in butter until onion is soft. Add zucchini, broth, and dill weed. Cover and simmer 15-20 minutes. Stir in yogurt and mix well. Puree in blender and stir in salt and pepper to taste. Serve either hot or cold.

AVOCADO SOUP
(serves 6-8)

    4 ripe avocados, peeled and pitted
    4 cups cold chicken broth
    1/4 cup lime juice
    1 teaspoon salt
    pinch of pepper
    1 tablespoon onion, finely chopped
    1/8 teaspoon tabasco sauce
    parsley (or chives)

Blend avocados and broth in blender or food processor. Pour into a bowl and add remaining ingredients except parsley. Blend until mixture is smooth. Chill, covered, in the refrigerator for 1 hour. Serve in cold bowls, garnishing soup with a sprig of parsley or chopped chives.

RACEY, LACEY TOMATO SOUP
(serves 4)

    4 tablespoons butter
    2 tablespoons onion, finely chopped
    2 cloves garlic, minced
    2 tablespoons green chili, chopped
    1 10-3/4 ounce can condensed tomato soup
    1 soup can water
    2 tablespoons tequila
    1 avocado, peeled and sliced

Melt butter and sauté onion, garlic, and chili until tender. Add soup, water, and tequila. Heat, stirring occasionally. Garnish with sliced avocados.

MEXICAN VEGETABLE SOUP
(serves 10-12)

    8 cups water
    1 large beef shank crosscut (about 1 pound)
    1 cup dry split peas
    1 tablespoon salt
    3 cloves garlic, minced
    8 ounces chorizo, sliced
    3 medium tomatoes, peeled, seeded, and chopped
    2 medium carrots, chopped
    1 medium onion, chopped
    1/2 medium green pepper, chopped
    4 cups cooked elbow macaroni

In a large pot, combine water, beef shank, split peas, salt, and garlic. Bring to a boil. Reduce heat; simmer covered one hour. Remove beef shank. Cut meat off bone, dice, and return to kettle. Discard bone. Add chorizo, tomatoes, carrots, onion, and green pepper. Simmer covered 20 minutes. Add macaroni. Simmer covered 10 minutes more.

PINTO BEAN SOUP
(serves 6-8)

    4 cups cooked pinto beans (see index)
    1 medium onion, chopped
    2 cloves garlic, peeled and chopped
    1/2 teaspoon dried oregano
    2 green chilies, peeled and chopped
    1/2 cup longhorn cheddar cheese, grated

Combine beans, onion, garlic, oregano, and chili. Cook over low heat for 30 minutes, adding water as necessary to keep from burning. Put through a food mill and return to saucepan. Add water or enough liquid from bean pot to bring soup to your desired consistency (fairly thick). Heat a few more minutes.

MEXICAN MEATBALL SOUP
(serves 10-12)

Meatballs

    1/2 pound ground beef, lean
    1/2 pound ground lean pork
    2 eggs, beaten
    1 onion, chopped
    2 garlic cloves, minced
    1 green chili, peeled and chopped
    1/2 teaspoon cumin
    1/4 teaspoon ground coriander
    1 teaspoon salt
    dash of pepper

Soup

    2 quarts beef broth
    1 medium onion, chopped
    2 medium carrots, diced
    1 large zucchini, peeled and cubed
    1/3 of a medium cabbage, shredded

MEXICAN MEATBALL SOUP (continued)

Combine meats, eggs, onion, garlic, chili, cumin, coriander, salt, and pepper in a large bowl. Form into small balls. In a large pot, bring beef broth to boiling. Place meatballs gently into broth. Bring to a boil again. Skim foam from broth surface. Add onion, carrots, and zucchini and return to boiling. Reduce heat and simmer uncovered 25 minutes. Add cabbage and cook 5 minutes longer or until all vegetables are tender.

GAZPACHO SOUP
(serves 8)

    3 large tomatoes, peeled and chopped
    1 bell pepper, chopped
    1 cucumber, peeled and chopped
    1 cup celery, chopped
    1 medium onion, chopped
    4 cups tomato juice
    green chili to taste
    garlic powder to taste
    4 tablespoons red wine vinegar
    3 tablespoons olive oil
    2 teaspoons salt
    1/2 teaspoon black pepper

All vegetables should be finely chopped. Combine all ingredients in a bowl and chill 6-8 hours. Serve with crackers, croutons, or French bread.

ZESTY CHEESE SOUP
(serves 8)

    3 tablespoons butter
    1 onion, finely chopped
    3 green onions, finely chopped
    1/2 teaspoon garlic powder
    4 ripe medium tomatoes, chopped

ZESTY CHEESE SOUP (continued)

1 4-ounce can green chili, chopped
2 tablespoons cilantro, chopped
1 cup water
1 teaspoon salt
1/8 teaspoon pepper
1 quart milk
2 cups monterey jack cheese, grated
1 cup sharp cheddar cheese, grated
1/4 pound butter

Melt butter and sauté onion, green onions, and garlic. Onions should be tender, not browned. Add tomatoes and simmer for 15 minutes. Stir in chili, cilantro, water, salt, and pepper. Keep warm. In another large saucepan, combine milk, cheeses, and butter. Melt ingredients over medium heat, stirring frequently. Add tomato mixture to cheese mixture. Stir over medium heat until mixture comes to boiling point, no longer. Serve hot.

TORTILLA CHICKEN SOUP
(serves 6-8)

1 dozen small corn tortillas
vegetable oil
1 large onion
5 cups chicken broth
6 ounces tomato sauce
1 8-ounce can tomatoes, peeled and diced
2 cloves garlic, minced
dash of hot pepper sauce
3 cups cheddar cheese, grated

Cut tortillas into strips and deep fry in oil until golden brown. Drain well on paper towels. Heat small amount of oil in saucepan and sauté onions until limp. To onions, add broth, tomato sauce, tomatoes, garlic, and hot pepper sauce. Simmer 30 minutes. Place half the tortillas in the soup. Use the remainder instead of crackers. Top with cheese.

CHILI CHICKEN SOUP
(serves 4)

>   4 cups chicken broth
>   2 cups cooked chicken, diced
>   salt and pepper to taste
>   1/2 cup green chili, chopped
>   2 cups cooked thin noodles

In a large saucepan, combine all ingredients except noodles and bring to a boil. Simmer for 20 minutes. Add noodles to soup and ladle out soup and noodles into individual bowls.

CHICKEN AND CABBAGE SOUP
(serves 8)

>   2 cups chicken broth
>   2 cups raw green cabbage, shredded
>   2 cans condensed cream of chicken soup
>   1 soup can water
>   1-1/2 cups green chili, chopped
>   2 cups cooked chicken, chopped

In a saucepan, heat broth and cabbage to boiling. Simmer 5 minutes. Remove from heat and add cream of chicken soup blended with water, chili, and chicken. Stir until smooth and return to heat. Simmer 10 minutes, stirring occasionally.

CAULIFLOWER SALAD
(serves 4)

    1 head cauliflower
    1/2 cup vegetable oil
    1/4 cup wine vinegar
    1/4 teaspoon salt
    1 tablespoon parsley
    1 tablespoon pimento, chopped
    1 hard boiled egg, chopped

Separate cauliflower into bite-sized flowers. Cook in boiling salted water until almost tender. Do not overcook. Drain. Combine oil, vinegar, salt, parsley, and pimento and stir thoroughly. Pour over cauliflower. Add egg and toss lightly. Chill to serve.

MACARONI AND CHEESE SALAD
(serves 4)

    1 cup macaroni, uncooked
    1 teaspoon salt
    1 teaspoon vegetable oil
    1/2 cup canned peas, drained
    2 tablespoons red onion, finely chopped
    1 cup small curd cottage cheese
    1/2 cup mayonnaise
    1/2 cup cooked carrots, diced
    4 tablespoons green chili, chopped

Cook macaroni in boiling salted water until tender. Drain and cool. In a bowl, combine macaroni and remaining ingredients. Toss gently but thoroughly. Chill and serve.

EGGPLANT SALAD
(serves 4)

    1 large eggplant
    olive oil
    1/4 cup green chili, chopped
    1/2 cup bell pepper, chopped
    1 tablespoon parsley
    2 large tomatoes, chopped
    2 tablespoons lime juice
    2 tablespoons vegetable oil
    1/2 teaspoon garlic powder
    salt and pepper
    lettuce leaves

Wash eggplant and slice into 1/4-inch slices. Brush both sides of each slice with olive oil and bake on cookie sheet at 350° until fork tender. Peel and chop. Add chili, bell pepper, parsley, and tomatoes to eggplant and toss. Add lime juice, oil, garlic powder, salt, and pepper. Toss lightly. Cover and refrigerate. Serve on bed of lettuce.

SOUTHWESTERN POTATO SALAD
(serves 12)

    8 large potatoes, peeled
    1-1/2 cups mayonnaise
    4 tablespoons milk
    1/2 cup green chili, chopped
    1/2 large onion, finely chopped
    1-1/2 cups monterey jack cheese, grated
    2 teaspoons lemon juice
    salt and pepper to taste

Cook potatoes in boiling salted water until done. Drain and cool. Cut into small cubes. Blend mayonnaise and milk. Set aside. Combine potatoes, chili, onion, and 2/3 of cheese. Sprinkle with lemon juice. Add salt and pepper. Pour mayonnaise mixture over salad. Toss gently. Place in serving bowl and top with remaining cheese.

MAIN DISHES

CHORIZO (MEXICAN SAUSAGE)
(yields 1 pound)

    1 pound ground lean pork
    1 teaspoon salt
    2 tablespoons chili powder
    1/2 teaspoon oregano
    1/4 teaspoon cumin
    2 large garlic cloves
    1/4 teaspoon pepper
    2 tablespoons vinegar

Mix all ingredients together thoroughly, cover tightly, and refrigerate 24 hours. Chorizo may be stored in refrigerator 3 or 4 days before cooking. To cook, form into patties or crumble and fry without oil over medium heat for 15-20 minutes.

GREEN CHILI STEW
(serves 6)

    2 pounds lean pork or beef, cubed
    1 cup flour
    4 tablespoons vegetable oil
    4 ripe medium tomatoes, chopped (or 1
      16-ounce can whole peeled tomatoes)
    1 large onion, chopped
    6-8 green chilies
    2 teaspoons salt
    1/2 teaspoon pepper
    1/4 teaspoon cumin
    2 cloves garlic
    1 teaspoon accent
    5 medium potatoes, peeled and quartered

GREEN CHILI STEW (continued)

In bag, shake meat and flour until meat is well coated. In heavy pot, brown meat in hot oil. Add remaining ingredients with the exception of the potatoes. Add enough water to cover and simmer for 2-1/2 hours. Add potatoes and continue to simmer until meat and vegetables are tender, about 45 minutes.

POSOLE
(serves 12)

    2 pounds lean pork or beef, cubed
    3 quarts water
    1/2 tablespoon salt
    1 pound posole
    1 medium onion, minced
    2 cloves garlic, minced
    6 red chili pods
    1 pint red chili sauce

Place meat in large kettle and cover with water. Add salt and bring to a boil. Reduce heat and simmer until meat is tender (about 1-1/2 hours). Cool and shred meat. Reserve meat broth, skimming off fat. Wash posole thoroughly, rinsing several times. Place posole in large kettle, covering with reserved broth. Bring to boil, lower heat to medium, and cook until posole has popped. Add more water if necessary. Combine meat, posole, garlic, onion, and chili pods and simmer at least 1/2 hour. Serve in bowls with heated red chili sauce on the side, if desired. This is a traditional holiday treat.

TACOS
(serves 4)

Shell

1 dozen corn tortillas
vegetable oil

In hot oil in small frying pan, fry one tortilla at a time for about 30 seconds. With tongs, fold half of tortilla over to form an envelope shape. Fry until crisp on one side; then turn and fry the other side. If softer shells are desired, fry just until set but not crisp. Drain each on paper towels. Fill each taco shell with filling; keep warm in oven until served.

Filling

1-1/2 pounds ground beef
salt and pepper to taste
1 can taco sauce or salsa (see index)
cheddar cheese, grated
lettuce, grated
tomatoes, chopped
onion, chopped (optional)
guacamole (optional)
sour cream (optional)

Brown beef, add salt and pepper, and drain well. Fill each taco shell with the browned beef and add 1 teaspoon taco sauce to each. (Sauce may be stirred into browned beef if desired.) Add grated cheese, lettuce, tomatoes, and whatever options you choose to each taco and serve immediately. For a party, serve condiments separately and allow each person to add their own ingredients.

Variations: Chicken, pork, or beans may be used instead of beef. Imagination and taste determine what goes in a taco!

TEXAS TACOS
(serves 4)

    1 dozen corn tortillas
    vegetable oil
    2 pounds ground beef
    1/2 onion, chopped
    1 can ranch-style beans
    1 teaspoon chili powder
    salt and pepper to taste
    1 pound longhorn cheddar cheese, grated
    taco sauce (optional)

In hot oil in small frying pan, lightly fry tortillas, one at a time, just until soft, about 30 seconds. Drain on paper towels. Brown ground beef and onion and drain well. With fork, mash beans in their own liquid. Combine meat, mashed beans, chili powder, salt, and pepper and mix well. Place a tablespoon of the mixture in the center of each tortilla, top with mound of cheese, and roll up into a tube. Fasten with toothpick and fry in hot oil, a few at a time, until crisp. Drain on paper towels, keep warm in oven, and serve hot with additional cheese and taco sauce, if desired.

TAQUITAS
(serves 4)

    1 dozen corn tortillas
    vegetable oil
    1-1/2 pounds ground beef
    salt and pepper to taste
    1 jar picante sauce or salsa (see index)
    2 cups longhorn cheddar cheese, grated

Lightly fry each corn tortilla in small amount of oil just until soft, about 30 seconds. Drain on paper towels. Brown beef and drain well. Add salt, pepper, 1/2 cup picante sauce, and cheese and stir well. Place meat mixture down the center of each tortilla. Roll up into a tube and fasten with

TAQUITAS (continued)

toothpicks. Push ends in slightly to seal. Fry in hot oil until crisp. Drain on paper towels and keep warm in oven until ready to serve. For added spice, serve a dish of warm picante sauce for "dipping".

TACO SALAD
(serves 6-8)

- 2 pounds ground beef
- 2 tablespoons onion, minced
- salt and pepper to taste
- 1 package corn chips
- 1 can ranch-style beans, drained
- 4 fresh tomatoes, chopped
- 1 pound longhorn cheddar cheese, grated
- 1 can taco sauce
- shredded lettuce, guacamole, sour cream (optional)

Brown beef and onion. Drain well. Add salt and pepper. Layer baking dish with corn chips, beef mixture, beans, tomatoes, cheese, and taco sauce. Repeat layers. Serve immediately. Top with lettuce, guacamole, and sour cream if desired.

CARNE ADOVADA
(serves 6)

- 2 pounds lean pork, cubed or in strips
- 1 teaspoon salt
- 2 cups red chili sauce (see index)
- 1 clove garlic, minced
- 1 teaspoon oregano
- longhorn cheddar cheese, grated (optional)

CARNE ADOVADA (continued)

Sprinkle meat with salt. Stir garlic and oregano into red chili sauce. Pour over meat and marinate in refrigerator overnight. Bake at 350° for 1 hour or until pork is tender. Serve as a stew or wrap in flour tortilla as a burrito, topped with red chili sauce and cheese.

TAMALES
(yields 12 dozen)

Meat Filling

- 10 pounds lean beef or pork
- 5 cloves garlic
- 6 tablespoons lard
- 6 tablespoons flour
- 6 cups red chili sauce (see index)
- salt

Simmer meat and 2 garlic cloves in a very large pot, covered with as much water as possible. When tender, at least 2 hours, cool, and shred meat and reserve all of broth. Meat should be prepared a day in advance to allow time for cooling. Refrigerate both meat and broth overnight. In large pot, fry 3 cloves garlic in lard. Add flour and brown slightly, stirring constantly. Add 6 cups red chili sauce and about 4-6 cups reserved broth. Add broth gradually to obtain the proper consistency, which should be that of a medium spaghetti sauce, not very watery. Simmer for 10 minutes. Remove 3 cups and set aside. Add the shredded meat to the chili sauce and simmer an additional 15 minutes. Add salt to taste. Set aside to cool while preparing masa.

TAMALES (continued)

Masa

3 pounds corn husks
1-1/2 pounds lard
5 pounds fresh masa or packaged masa harina
3 cups reserved red chili sauce mixture
beef broth

Separate corn husks and soak in warm water at least 20 minutes, preferably overnight. Wash each husk thoroughly under running water, removing all silk. Drain well on lots of newspapers. Place lard in electric mixer and cream for 20 minutes. If fresh masa is not available, use packaged masa harina according to directions. Combine masa and creamed lard. Mix well with hands, breaking up all lumps. Add the 3 cups reserved red chili sauce mixture. Gradually add beef broth, still mixing with hands until mixture is a good spreading consistency (about like peanut butter).

Using clean husks, spread masa mixture over bottom half of each husk (the widest half), just thick enough so you can't see through it (about 2 tablespoons). Spread to within 1/2 inch of sides and 1/4 inch from bottom. Top with generous tablespoon of meat mixture. Amount will depend on the size of the husk. Fold one side of the husk over the center, then the other side, and then fold the top down. Place seam down on cookie sheet. Repeat until cookie sheet is filled with one layer of tamales. Place in freezer about 30 minutes or until firm. Then place tamales into freezer bags or foil, usually 1 dozen per package. Freeze for future use. Continue until all ingredients are used.

If using tamales on day of preparation, do not freeze. Place standing up in steamer or on tray in large pot. Place 1-2 inches of water in bottom of pot, and <u>cover tightly</u>. Steam until masa is cooked (it will be firm), usually about 1 hour. Add more water as necessary to bottom of pot, being careful

TAMALES (continued)

not to let it boil away. To cook frozen tamales, do not thaw. Steam in the same way, although the time may vary. Serve tamales with a side dish of red chili sauce as garnish.

CHILI CON CARNE AMERICANO
(serves 12)

- 4 pounds ground beef
- 2 large onions, finely chopped
- 6 pounds canned tomatoes
- 3 pounds canned pinto beans (reserve liquid)
- 1 pound canned tomato sauce
- 1/8 cup sugar
- 3 tablespoons chili powder
- 1-1/2 tablespoons salt

In large pan, brown beef and onions. Drain well. Add tomatoes, liquid from beans, tomato sauce, and seasonings. Simmer uncovered for 1-1/2 hours. Add beans and simmer uncovered for 15 minutes.

CHILI CON CARNE DE ALBUQUERQUE

- 3-1/2 pounds stew beef
- 5 tablespoons oil
- 1 large onion, minced
- 2 cloves garlic, minced
- 4 tablespoons chili powder
- 1-1/2 teaspoons oregano
- 1-1/2 teaspoons ground cumin
- 1 teaspoon crushed red pepper
- 2 cups beef broth
- 1 large can tomatoes
- 1 6-ounce can tomato paste
- 1 tablespoon sugar
- 1-2 tablespoons yellow cornmeal

CHILI CON CARNE DE ALBUQUERQUE (continued)

Sear meat in 3 tablespoons hot oil in large heavy pot. Brown on all sides (3-4 minutes). Remove meat to bowl. To pot, add 3 tablespoons oil, onion, and garlic and sauté until onion is transparent. Stir in chili powder, oregano, cumin, and red peppers and mix well. Add broth, tomatoes and liquid, tomato paste, salt, and sugar and mix well. Break up tomatoes with spoon. Return meat to pot; cover and simmer 1 hour. Uncover and simmer 1 hour more or until meat is tender. Cool, cover, and refrigerate overnight. To serve, bring to boil, then simmer for 15 minutes. If mixture is thin, do not cover. When hot, thicken if desired by sprinkling in 1 tablespoon of cornmeal and mixing well. Add 1 tablespoon more if needed.

CHILI CON CARNE ROJO
(serves 4)

> 1-1/2 pounds lean stew beef, cubed
> 4 tablespoons flour
> 3 tablespoons vegetable oil
> 1 quart red chili sauce (see index)
> 2 garlic cloves, minced
> 1 teaspoon salt
> 1 teaspoon oregano

Dredge beef in flour and brown in oil. Add red chili sauce, garlic, salt, and oregano and stir. Simmer at least 1 hour or until meat is tender. If liquid is too thick, thin with water. Serve with flour tortillas.

PORK CHILI CON CARNE
(serves 4)

    2 pounds lean pork, cubed
    1 garlic clove
    dash oregano
    red chili sauce (see index)

Place cubed pork in a small amount of water. Add garlic clove and oregano and simmer 1 hour. Add more water only if necessary to prevent burning. Add red chili sauce to cover and continue cooking until meat is tender. Serve with warm flour tortillas.

AUTHENTIC CHEESE ENCHILADAS
(serves 4)

    1 dozen corn tortillas
    vegetable oil
    3 cups longhorn cheddar cheese, grated
    1 cup onion, diced
    4 cups red or green chili sauce (see index - optional)
    lettuce, grated
    4 fried eggs (optional)

Lightly fry tortillas, one at a time, in hot oil just enough to soften, about 30 seconds. Drain on paper towels. Sprinkle cheese down center of each tortilla, top with diced onion, and roll tortilla into a tube. Arrange on oven-proof dishes, top with red or green chili sauce if desired, cover with more cheese, and place in warm oven until cheese melts. Garnish with fried egg (This is a delicious traditional garnish!) and grated lettuce.

CHICKEN ENCHILADAS
(serves 4)

Prepare as above, adding diced chicken to each tortilla. Warm the chicken before filling tortillas.

ENCHILADAS - RED OR GREEN
(serves 4)

    1 dozen corn tortillas
    vegetable oil
    4 cups red or green chili sauce (see index)
    1 pound longhorn cheddar cheese, grated
    4 tablespoons onion, minced
    1 pound ground beef, browned and drained (optional)
    lettuce, grated (optional)
    tomatoes, diced (optional)
    4 fried eggs (optional)

In small frying pan, fry tortillas in 1/2 inch hot oil, one at a time to soften, only about 30 seconds. Drain on paper towels. Place 1 tortilla on individual serving dish, spread with red or green chili sauce, sprinkle with meat if desired, and top with cheese and onion. Repeat layers, using 4 dishes, 3 layers per dish. Keep warm in oven until served. Serve with refried beans, rice, or in a combination plate with tacos, etc.

SOUR CREAM ENCHILADAS
(serves 4)

    1 pound ground beef
    1/4 cup onion, minced
    1/4 teaspoon salt
    1/8 teaspoon pepper
    1 dozen corn tortillas
    vegetable oil
    1 pound cheddar cheese, grated

SOUR CREAM ENCHILADAS (continued)

    4 cups green chili sauce (see index)
    1 cup sour cream

Brown meat with onions and drain well. Add salt and pepper. In 1/2 inch hot oil, fry one tortilla at a time until soft, about 30 seconds. Drain on paper towels. Spoon meat mixture down center of each tortilla. Top with cheese. Roll tortilla into a tube and place seam down in a lightly greased baking dish. Add sour cream to green chili sauce and blend. Pour over rolled tortillas. Top with more cheese. Bake at 350° for 15-20 minutes or until bubbly.

EASY ENCHILADA CASSEROLE
(serves 4)

    1 package corn chips
    3 cups cooked chicken or turkey, cubed
    1 4-ounce can green chili
    1/4 cup bell peppers, diced
    1/4 cup onion, diced
    1 can cream of mushroom or cream of chicken
       soup
    2 cups longhorn cheddar cheese, grated
    sour cream (optional)

Line baking dish with corn chips. Spread them with a layer of chicken, chili, and vegetables. Repeat layers. Dilute soup with 1/2 can water and pour over layers. Top with grated cheese and sour cream if desired and bake at 350° for 45 minutes.

BAKED CHICKEN ENCHILADA CASSEROLE
(serves 6)

    1 dozen corn tortillas
    vegetable oil

BAKED CHICKEN ENCHILADA CASSEROLE
(continued)

1 can cream of chicken soup or cream of mushroom soup
1 can cheddar cheese soup
3 cups cooked chicken or turkey pieces
1 cup green chili, chopped
1 cup sour cream
1/2 pound longhorn cheddar cheese, grated

Lightly fry tortillas in 1/4 inch hot oil just until soft, about 30 seconds. Drain on paper towels. In saucepan combine soups, chicken, chili, and sour cream. Heat on low flame, stirring until blended. Line a baking dish with half of the tortillas. Add half the soup mixture and half of the grated cheese. Repeat layers, topping with cheese. Bake at 350° for about 30 minutes until bubbly.

BEEF ENCHILADA CASSEROLE
(serves 6-8)

1 onion, chopped
1 bell pepper, chopped
2 tablespoons butter
2 pounds lean ground beef
2 10-ounce cans green chili enchilada sauce
2 4-ounce cans green chilies, chopped
1 dozen corn tortillas
vegetable oil
1 pound sharp cheddar cheese, grated

Sauté onion and bell pepper in butter in large frying pan. Add beef and cook until browned. Drain excess grease. Stir in enchilada sauce and green chilies and heat slowly. Fry corn tortillas, one at a time in 1/2 inch hot oil, just until softened, about 30 seconds. Drain on paper towels. In large greased casserole, layer 6 tortillas, half of meat mixture, and cheese. Repeat layers, topping with cheese, and bake at 350° for 15-20 minutes or until bubbly and cheese melts.

CHILIES RELLENOS (STUFFED GREEN CHILIES)
(serves 4)

    12 green chilies
    1 pound longhorn cheddar cheese
    vegetable oil

Batter:

    3 eggs
    1-1/2 tablespoons flour
    1/4 teaspoon salt

Slit chilies just enough to remove seeds and insert a strip of cheese 1/4 inch thick and 2-3 inches long. Carefully slip cheese into each chili and secure with toothpick. Dry on paper towels. Separate eggs. Beat yolks and add flour and salt, mixing well. Beat egg whites until stiff. Add yolk mixture to whites and beat until smooth. Dip chilies into batter and coat well. Fry in hot oil until golden brown. Drain and serve warm with a side dish of green chili sauce and topped with more cheese, if desired.

BAKED CHILIES RELLENOS
(serves 4)

    12 green chilies
    1 pound longhorn cheddar cheese

Batter:

    4 eggs
    4 tablespoons flour
    1/2 teaspoon salt
    3/4 teaspoon baking powder

BAKED CHILIES RELLENOS (continued)

Carefully slit top of chilies, remove seeds, and insert 1/4 inch thick strip of cheese, 2-3 inches long. Place chilies in lightly greased baking dish. For batter, separate eggs. Beat yolks and add flour, salt, and baking powder, mixing well. Beat egg whites until stiff. Fold whites into yolk mixture. Pour batter over chilies and bake at 325° until batter is lightly browned and knife inserted in center comes out clean. Top with grated cheese and serve hot.

EGGPLANT CASSEROLE
(serves 6)

- 1 pound ground beef
- 1 cup onion, chopped
- 1-1/2 cups eggplant, peeled and coarsely chopped
- 1 cup potato, peeled and coarsely chopped
- 1/2 cup tomato sauce
- 1 teaspoon chili powder
- 3/4 teaspoon nutmeg
- 1/2 teaspoon salt
- 1/2 teaspoon garlic powder
- 1/4 cup parmesan cheese, grated
- 2 eggs
- 1 cup plain yogurt

Brown beef and onion. Drain off excess fat. Stir in eggplant, potato, tomato sauce, chili powder, nutmeg, salt, and garlic powder. Simmer covered for 20 minutes or until potatoes and eggplant are tender. Stir in cheese. Spoon into 1-1/2 quart casserole. Beat eggs and yogurt together and spoon onto top of eggplant mixture. Bake uncovered at 350° for 30-35 minutes or until set.

GUACAMOLE-TOMATO SALAD
(serves 6)

    6 large tomatoes
    salt
    1/2 cup onion, finely chopped
    2 cans green chili, chopped
    2 teaspoons lemon juice
    2 ripe avocados
    3 slices bacon, cooked crisp

Cut 1/2-inch slice from stem end of each tomato. Scoop out centers and chop finely. Sprinkle insides of tomatoes with salt. Turn upside down on paper towels to drain and refrigerate. Combine onion, chili, and lemon juice and chopped tomatoes. Cover and refrigerate. Peel and pit avocados. Mash and stir into chopped tomato mixture. Spoon mixture into tomato cups; top with crumbled bacon. Arrange on lettuce leaves on platter and pass remaining guacamole as garnish.

GREEN CHILI-CHEESE BAKE
(serves 12)

    12 slices white bread, trimmed, buttered, and cubed
    1 pound longhorn cheddar cheese, grated
    1 pound bacon, fried and crumbled
    chopped parsley
    1 4-ounce can green chili, chopped
    6 eggs, beaten
    4 cups milk
    1-1/2 teaspoons onion, finely chopped
    1/4 teaspoon salt
    pepper
    1/2 teaspoon dry mustard

Place cubed, buttered bread in 9 x 13 inch greased pan. Sprinkle with 3/4 of the cheese, all of the bacon, parsley, and green chilies. Mix eggs, milk, onion, and seasonings. Pour over other ingredients

GREEN CHILI-CHEESE BAKE (continued)

in baking dish. Mix very lightly with fork. Sprinkle remainder of cheese on top. Refrigerate overnight to set. Bake uncovered at 350° for 45 minutes.

CHALUPAS
(serves 4)

    1 dozen corn tortillas
    vegetable oil
    choice of fillings
    longhorn cheddar cheese, grated
    grated lettuce, chopped tomatoes, guacamole,
      sour cream (options)

Place tortillas, one at a time, in 1 inch of hot oil. Hold a large wooden spoon in the center of the tortilla and it will curl up around the handle of the spoon, forming a "cup". Fry until tortilla is crisp and holds its shape. Turn so all sides are cooked evenly. Drain on paper towels. Fill with carne adovada, chicken, beans, or any filling that appeals to you. See index for ideas. Any taco, burrito, or enchilada filling is delicious served this way. Top with grated cheese and any option of your choice. This is a favorite company recipe - try it!

EASY MEATLESS CASSEROLE
(serves 4)

    1 dozen corn tortillas (or 6 ounces corn or
      tortilla chips)
    vegetable oil
    1 can cream of mushroom soup
    1 can cheddar cheese soup
    1 4-ounce can green chili, chopped
    2 tablespoons onion, minced
    1/2 pound longhorn cheddar cheese, grated
    sour cream

EASY MEATLESS CASSEROLE (continued)

In hot oil, fry tortillas about 30 seconds, just until soft. Drain on paper towels. Combine undiluted soups and green chili and heat until well mixed. Arrange a layer of tortillas (or chips) in bottom of casserole. Add 1/2 soup mixture and layer with 1/2 of the cheese and onion. Repeat layers, topping with cheese and sour cream dollops. Bake at 350° for 20 minutes or until bubbly.

SHRIMP OLÉ
(serves 4-6)

 1-1/2 pounds raw shrimp, shelled and deveined
 3 tablespoons peanut oil
 1 onion, sliced
 1 clove garlic, minced
 4 stalks of celery, chopped
 1-1/2 tablespoons flour
 2-1/2 cups canned tomatoes
 1 bay leaf
 1/2 teaspoon thyme
 1 tablespoon chili powder
 1/2 pound fresh mushrooms, sliced and sautéed in butter
 2 pimentos, chopped
 dash salt and pepper

Wash and dry the shrimp thoroughly. In a large skillet, heat the oil and add the onions, garlic, and half the celery and cook until tender. Sprinkle in the flour and cook, stirring constantly until mixture is lightly browned. Add the rest of the ingredients, except the shrimp and celery, and cook for 10 minutes. Then add the shrimp and remaining celery and simmer another 10 minutes.

BARBECUE SHRIMP
(serves 6)

    1 cup butter, softened
    2 tablespoons lemon juice
    1 teaspoon chili powder
    1/4 teaspoon dried oregano
    1/4 teaspoon salt
    1/8 teaspoon pepper
    1 clove garlic, minced
    2 pounds large raw shrimp, peeled and deveined

Cream butter with remaining ingredients except shrimp. Divide shrimp equally on 6 pieces of heavy-duty aluminum foil. Top with seasoning mixture. Fold foil around shrimp and seal tightly. Place pockets directly on hot coals. Cook 5-7 minutes. Serve on a bed of rice.

SHRIMP SALAD
(serves 4)

    4 cups water
    1 tablespoon salt
    1 tablespoon vinegar
    1 bay leaf
    1 celery branch
    1 pound shrimp
    1/4 cup green chili, chopped
    1 small tomato
    4 green onions, chopped
    2 tablespoons cilantro leaves, chopped
    1 tablespoon lime juice
    salt and pepper
    4 lettuce leaves
    4 tablespoons mayonnaise
    4 lime wedges

Combine water, salt, vinegar, bay leaf, and celery. Bring to a boil. Add shrimp in shells, return to boil, and then simmer until shrimp turns pink,

SHRIMP SALAD (continued)

about 1-3 minutes. Drain and reserve liquid. Peel and devein shrimp. Place in bowl, cover with reserved liquid, and chill. Before serving, drain shrimp and mix with chili, tomato, onion, cilantro, and lime juice. Add salt and pepper to taste. Serve on bed of lettuce accompanied by 1 tablespoon of mayonnaise per serving. Garnish with lime wedge.

GARLIC-FLAVORED SOLE
(serves 2-4)

    1 small lemon
    1 pound fillet of sole
    salt and pepper
    1/4 cup olive oil
    3 garlic cloves, chopped
    1/4 cup vegetable oil
    fresh parsley, chopped

Squeeze lemon juice over fish. Sprinkle with salt and pepper. Heat olive oil and garlic in skillet until garlic starts to brown. Keep garlic oil warm. In a large skillet, heat vegetable oil and add fish. Fry until sole flakes easily, 7-10 minutes. Turn once. Spoon some of the garlic oil onto each portion of fish. Garnish with parsley.

ARROZ CON POLLO (RICE WITH CHICKEN)
(serves 8)

    3 whole chicken breasts
    1-1/2 quarts water
    1 large onion
    2 carrots, peeled
    2 celery stalks
    salt and pepper to taste
    1 8-1/2 ounce can peas, drained

ARROZ CON POLLO (continued)

20 large Spanish-style green olives
3/4 teaspoon dried leaf oregano, crushed
1 teaspoon salt
pepper to taste
1 tablespoon vegetable oil
1 cup uncooked rice
1 cup canned tomatoes

Place chicken breasts in a large pot. Add water, onions, carrots, celery, salt, and pepper. Cover, bring to a boil, then reduce heat and simmer until tender, about 1 hour. Drain chicken, reserving broth. Remove chicken in strips from breasts. Combine chicken, peas, olives, oregano, salt, and pepper. Set aside. Heat oil in large skillet. Add rice and sauté until lightly browned. Pour rice into casserole, add chicken mixture and tomatoes, and mix gently. Pour on enough reserved broth to cover. Bake covered about 1 hour at 350°.

GREEN CHILI-CHICKEN DIVAN
(serves 4-6)

4 chicken breasts
1 onion
2 carrots, peeled
1 celery stalk
salt and pepper to taste
2 10-ounce packages frozen broccoli or 1 large bunch fresh broccoli
2 cans cream of chicken soup
1 cup mayonnaise
1 teaspoon lemon juice
1/2 teaspoon curry powder
1/4 cup green chili, chopped
1/2 cup sharp cheddar cheese, grated

In pot, cover chicken with water, salt, pepper. Add onion, carrots, and celery and simmer until meat is done, about 1 hour. Remove bones and skin. Cook broccoli according to package directions

GREEN CHILI-CHICKEN DIVAN (continued)

or, if using fresh, cook in boiling salted water until tender. Drain. Arrange stalks in a greased baking dish and place a portion of chicken on top of each stalk for easy serving. Combine soup, mayonnaise, lemon juice, curry powder, and chili. Pour over chicken. Sprinkle with cheese and bake at 350° for 30 minutes.

MEXICAN CHICKEN
(serves 4)

>   4 chicken breasts
>   1 tablespoon butter
>   1/2 teaspoon salt
>   1/4 teaspoon pepper
>   1/4 teaspoon garlic powder
>   2 teaspoons ground cumin
>   1 teaspoon chili powder
>   4 tablespoons butter or margarine

Arrange chicken in buttered baking dish. Combine spices and sprinkle over chicken pieces. Place 1 tablespoon of butter over each breast. Bake at 350° for 45 minutes or until chicken is done.

OVEN-FRIED CHICKEN

>   1 2-1/2 to 3 pound frying chicken pieces
>   1 package taco seasoning mix
>   1/2 cup melted butter
>   1 cup bread crumbs

Blend taco seasoning mix with melted butter. Roll chicken in mixture and then roll in bread crumbs. Bake at 350° for 45 minutes. Turn and bake 15 minutes more or until done.

CHICKEN AND GREEN CHILI
(serves 4)

    1 large cut-up fryer
    2 carrots, peeled
    1 clove garlic
    salt to taste
    water
    1 medium onion, minced
    2 tablespoons vegetable oil
    1 cup green chili sauce (see index)

Place chicken pieces, carrots, celery, garlic, and salt in large pot. Cover with water and simmer until chicken is tender, about 1 hour. Remove from pot and place in large skillet. In small skillet, sauté onion in oil until transparent. Add green chili sauce and bring to a boil. Pour over chicken and simmer 1/2 hour. Serve on a bed of rice.

CHICKEN AND RICE CASSEROLE
(serves 4-6)

    1-1/3 cups minute rice
    1 can cream of mushroom soup
    1 envelope onion soup mix
    1-1/4 cups boiling water
    1/4 cup green chili
    1 small can mushrooms
    1 cut-up fryer
    2 sticks butter, melted
    1 teaspoon salt
    1/4 teaspoon pepper
    1 tablespoon paprika
    1/4 cup sherry

Combine first 6 ingredients and pour into baking dish. Place chicken on top of mixture and brush with butter, salt, pepper, and paprika mixture. Cover tightly and bake at 350° for 1 hour. Add sherry and bake 30 minutes more.

CHILI-CHICKEN ROLL UPS
(serves 6-8)

    6 boned chicken breasts
    3/4 cup unsifted flour
    3 beaten eggs
    1-1/2 cups bread crumbs
    vegetable oil

Herb butter:

    1 cup butter, softened
    1/2 teaspoon chili powder
    1/2 teaspoon cumin
    1/2 teaspoon oregano
    1/4 teaspoon salt

Mix herb butter ingredients and, on foil, shape into a 6-inch square. Freeze about 40 minutes until firm. Wash and dry chicken, remove skin, and cut each breast in half. Place pieces between wax paper and pound to 1/4 inch thick. Cut frozen butter into 12 parts and put one part in center of each chicken piece. Fold long sides of chicken over butter, then fold ends over so no butter is showing. Secure with toothpicks and roll in flour. Dip in beaten eggs and then in bread crumbs. Refrigerate 1 hour to chill. In heavy pan or deep fryer, heat 3 inches of oil to 360°. Add chicken a few at a time and fry until deep brown (about 6 minutes). Drain. Keep warm and serve immediately. To freeze, cool, wrap well, and store until needed. To serve, do not defrost. Bake uncovered at 350° for 30 minutes.

TURKEY-TORTILLA CASSEROLE
(serves 4)

    3 cups cooked turkey pieces
    6 corn tortillas
    1 4-ounce can green chili
    1 can cream of chicken soup
    1 can cheddar cheese soup

TURKEY-TORTILLA CASSEROLE (continued)

    1/2 cup milk
    1/2 pound sharp cracker barrel cheese, grated
    salt to taste
    1/2 onion, minced

Cut tortillas into 1-inch strips. Remove seeds from chilies and cut into strips. Mix undiluted soups with milk, salt, and onion. Grease large casserole and sprinkle lightly with water. Arrange layers of tortillas, turkey, chili, soup mixture, and cheese. Repeat, topping with cheese. Refrigerate 1 hour and then bake at 300° for 1 hour.

ALL-IN-ONE CASSEROLE
(serves 8)

    2 pounds lean ground beef
    4 medium potatoes, grated
    1-1/2 cups green chili, chopped
    1 large onion, chopped
    2 cloves garlic, minced
    2 teaspoons salt
    1-1/2 pounds canned tomatoes
    1 large bag corn chips
    1 pound longhorn cheddar cheese, grated

Brown meat in large pan. Drain well. To meat, add potatoes, chili, onion, garlic, salt, tomatoes, and 1-1/2 cups water. Stir to break up tomatoes; cover and simmer for 30 minutes. Layer casserole dish with half the corn chips and half the grated cheese. Layer chips with the meat mixture and top with remaining cheese and chips. Bake at 325° for 30 minutes.

SPINACH AND BEEF CASSEROLE
(serves 6)

    2 pounds ground beef
    1/2 cup onion, minced
    1 package taco seasoning mix
    1 cup water
    1 cup taco sauce
    1 dozen corn tortillas
    2 10-ounce packages frozen chopped spinach
    1 pound longhorn cheddar cheese, grated
    1 cup sour cream

Brown ground beef and onion and drain well. Add taco seasoning mix and water. Simmer for 5 minutes. Pour 1/2 cup taco sauce in bottom of casserole dish. Line with 6 tortillas. Cook spinach according to package directions, undercooking slightly. Drain well and add to beef mixture. Pour 1/2 mixture over tortillas; layer with 1/2 cheese, remaining tortillas, taco sauce, beef mixture, and cheese. Spoon sour cream on top. Cover and bake at 350° for 20 minutes. Uncover and bake another 10 minutes.

PORK AND RED CHILI
(serves 4)

    1 pound lean pork, cubed
    1 tablespoon vegetable oil
    1 tablespoon flour
    1 teaspoon salt
    2 cups red chili sauce (see index)
    1 clove garlic
    dash cumin
    dash oregano

Brown pork in vegetable oil. Add flour and salt and stir well. Add remaining ingredients; cover and simmer for 1 hour or until meat is tender. Serve with warm flour tortillas and beans.

GREEN CHILI STROGANOFF
(serves 4-6)

    3 tablespoons vegetable oil
    1 onion, diced
    1 clove garlic, diced
    1 4-ounce can sliced mushrooms
    2 pounds lean beef, cubed and coated with flour
    2 cups beef broth
    1 4-ounce can green chili, chopped
    1 cup sour cream
    1 large package noodles

Sauté onions, garlic, and mushrooms in oil. Add beef and brown slightly. Add beef broth; cover and simmer for 1-1/2 hours or until meat is tender. Add green chili and simmer 10 minutes longer. Remove from heat and stir in sour cream. Cook noodles according to package directions; drain well. Serve meat on hot noodles.

STEAK ROLL UPS
(serves 6)

    1-1/2 pounds round steak, 1/4 inch thick
    salt and pepper
    3 green chilies, peeled and seeded
    1/2 cup butter
    1 clove garlic, minced
    1 cup seasoned bread crumbs
    1 tablespoon parsley, chopped
    2 hard-boiled eggs, chopped
    1/4 cup parmesan cheese
    3/4 cup butter
    1 can condensed onion soup
    1/2 cup fresh mushrooms, chopped
    1 cup dry red wine

Pound steak until very thin; then cut into 6 long strips. Sprinkle with salt and pepper. Cut each chili in half and place 1/2 on each piece of meat.

STEAK ROLL UPS (continued)

Sauté garlic in 1/2 cup butter until golden brown. Add crumbs and sauté briefly until well coated. Stir in parsley, eggs, and parmesan cheese. Spoon mixture onto each piece of meat. Roll up and secure with toothpicks. Brown meat on all sides in remaining 3/4 cup butter. Add onion soup, mushrooms, and wine. Cover and simmer 1 hour or until meat is tender. Thicken pan juices to make gravy if desired and serve over noodles.

CARNE ASADA
(serves 4)

- 1-1/2 pounds sirloin steak
- 2 tablespoons vegetable oil
- 3/4 teaspoon dried leaf oregano, crushed
- 1/2 teaspoon salt
- 1/4 teaspoon pepper
- 1 tablespoon lime juice
- 2 teaspoons cider vinegar
- 2 orange slices

Place steak in shallow baking dish and brush each side with oil. Combine remaining ingredients except orange slices. Pour over steak, cover, and refrigerate several hours, turning occasionally. To cook, preheat charcoal grill. Drain meat, reserving marinade. Grill 3 to 4 minutes on each side, for medium rare. Spoon marinade over steak as it cooks. After turning once, garnish with orange slices and serve hot.

EMPAÑADAS

Filling

2-1/2 pounds lean beef, cubed
2 cups applesauce
1 cup raisins
1 cup brown sugar
1 teaspoon cinnamon
1/2 teaspoon ground cloves
1/2 cup piñon nuts or chopped pecans

Simmer meat until tender in just enough water to cover it. Reserve broth; shred meat. In large pot, combine shredded meat and remaining ingredients and enough reserved broth to moisten. Simmer about 15 minutes, adding more broth as needed to keep mixture moist. Cool thoroughly. While mixture cools, prepare dough.

Dough

1/2 cup sugar
1/4 cup butter or margarine
1 large egg
2-1/2 cups flour
1/8 teaspoon baking soda
1/2 teaspoon baking powder
1/4 teaspoon salt
vegetable oil

Blend sugar and butter. Add egg and mix well. Sift flour, baking soda, baking powder, and salt and add to butter mixture. Add warm water, a little at a time, and work into a soft dough. Divide into 4 portions and roll each on floured surface to 1/8 inch thick. Cut rounds with inverted glass or biscuit cutter. Fill with spoonful of meat mixture; fold over and seal well. Fry in hot oil (375°) until golden brown. May be frozen.

BURRITOS

A burrito is a flour tortilla filled with an assortment of meats, beans, cheeses, etc. The following recipes will give you some ideas, but use your imagination and use any mixture in this book that appeals to you! Top burritos with grated cheddar cheese for added appeal.

PORK BURRITOS
(serves 8)

    8 flour tortillas
    2 pounds lean pork
    water
    1 small onion
    1 large garlic clove
    1 teaspoon salt
    1/4 teaspoon dried crushed leaf oregano
    1/4 teaspoon cumin
    garlic salt
    1 can refried beans
    1 can salsa
    cheddar cheese, grated

Place meat in 3-quart saucepan and cover with water. Add onion, garlic, salt, oregano, and cumin. Bring to boil, reduce heat, cover, and simmer 2 hours or until meat is tender. Cool and shred.

Wrap flour tortillas in foil, seal, and warm in oven (or wrap in wax paper and warm in microwave). Place about 1/2 cup meat filling a little below center of each warmed tortilla. Add 3 tablespoons heated refried beans; top with 1 tablespoon of salsa. Fold sides of tortilla over filling. Fold top and bottom, enclosing filling completely. Top with warm salsa and grated cheese; place in oven to melt cheese and serve immediately.

CHICKEN BURRITOS
(serves 4)

    1 cup onion, chopped
    1 8-ounce can green chili, chopped
    2 tablespoons vegetable oil
    2 cups cooked chicken, shredded
    1 cup sour cream
    salt to taste
    4 flour tortillas
    longhorn cheddar cheese, grated

Sauté onion and green chili in oil until onion is transparent. Add the chicken, heat thoroughly, add sour cream and salt, and simmer for 5 minutes - do not let mixture boil. Fill center of each tortilla with mixture. Roll into a tube, secure with toothpick, and cover with grated cheese. Heat in oven at 350° for 5 minutes or until cheese melts. Serve with warm salsa, if desired.

CHIMICHANGAS (FRIED BURRITOS)
(serves 8)

    8 burritos prepared with any filling (carne adovada filling is especially delicious in a chimichanga - see index)
    vegetable oil
    lettuce, shredded (optional)
    8 tablespoons guacamole (optional)
    8 tablespoons sour cream (optional)
    longhorn cheddar cheese, grated

Seal burrito filling inside flour tortilla by folding all four sides tightly over center. Fry in hot oil until tortilla browns and starts crisping. Drain on paper towels; arrange on serving dish and top with options and cheese. Warm in oven until cheese melts.

FAJITAS
(serves 6)

Zesty Fajita Marinade

4 ounces liquid smoke
1 clove garlic, minced
juice of 1/2 lime
1-1/2 teaspoons crushed red chili pepper
1-1/2 teaspoons sugar
1/2 teaspoon onion, minced
1/8 teaspoon cayenne pepper (to taste)

Meat Filling

1-1/2 pounds round steak or 6 chicken breasts
1 onion, thinly sliced
2 bell peppers, diced
6 flour tortillas
1-1/2 cups cheddar cheese, grated
Garnishes: guacamole, sour cream,
   2 tomatoes chopped, salsa

Combine all ingredients for marinade. Slice beef or chicken into very thin strips, cover with marinade. Refrigerate at least 30 minutes, stirring a few times to make sure all meat is coated. Sauté meat and vegetables in the marinade about 10 minutes or until tender. Place portion of meat mixture in center of each warm tortilla, top with garnishes. Roll up each tortilla and serve immediately.

Fajitas are so easy to prepare and are such a trendy popular dish! Garnishes can be added or subtracted as desired and each person can create their own delicious combination. Use the zesty fajita marinade for down home-on-the-range flavor or try the following fabulous vaquero-lime recipe for a more subtle flavor. Preparations and cooking instructions remain the same, regardless of which marinade is used.

Vaquero-Lime Marinade

juice of 4 limes
2/3 cup olive oil
3 cloves garlic, minced
1-1/2 tablespoons dried cilantro
1/2 teaspoon each salt and pepper

EGG DISHES

CHORIZO AND EGGS
(serves 4)

    2 cups chorizo, crumbled (see index)
    4 flour tortillas, warmed
    8 eggs
    vegetable oil
    salt and pepper to taste
    4 tablespoons sour cream
    3/4 cup green chili sauce (optional)

Fry chorizo in skillet for 15-20 minutes. Beat eggs; add salt and pepper. Scramble eggs in oil-coated pan. Top each tortilla with eggs, chorizo, and sour cream. Green chili sauce may be poured over eggs and chorizo if desired.

CHILI AND MUSHROOM OMELET
(serves 6)

             Filling (six omelets)

    2 tablespoons butter
    1/2 cup green chilies, chopped
    1 small onion, chopped
    4 medium-sized mushrooms, sliced
    1/2 pound bacon, cooked and crumbled
    1/2 pound longhorn cheddar cheese, grated

             Omelets (one)

    2 eggs, beaten
    1 tablespoon cream
    1-1/2 tablespoons butter
    salt to taste

CHILI AND MUSHROOM OMELET (continued)

Melt butter in medium-sized skillet. Sauté chilies, onion, and mushrooms until all are tender. Add crumbled bacon. Combine eggs, cream, and salt. Melt butter in omelet pan or skillet with sloping sides. Add eggs, tilting pan until omelet is shiny and just moist on top. Remove from heat and spoon 1/2 cup of filling on bottom half of omelet. Top with grated cheese. Fold omelet in half and flip onto serving plate.

SPANISH OMELET
(serves 4)

> 2 tablespoons butter
> 6 eggs, beaten
> 1/4 cup milk
> salt and pepper to taste
> 1/2 cup cheddar cheese, grated
> 1/4 cup bell pepper, chopped
> 2 tablespoons minced onion
> 1/4 cup pimentos, chopped
> 1/2 cup green chili, chopped
> 1 cup ham, cubed

In large frying pan, melt butter. Beat eggs and milk together. Add salt and pepper and pour into pan. Cook for a few minutes to set eggs slightly. Tip pan, allowing eggs to run underneath set egg. While still slightly moist on top, add rest of ingredients. Cover and cook for a few minutes. When mixture is fairly well set, flip one half over. Cover and cook a few minutes more until fully set.

CHEESE QUICHE
(serves 4-6)

    baked pie crust
    1 cup longhorn cheddar cheese, grated
    1 cup monterey jack cheese, grated
    3 large eggs, beaten
    1 teaspoon salt
    1/8 teaspoon pepper
    1 teaspoon chili powder
    1-1/2 cups half and half
    1 4-ounce can green chili, chopped
    1/2 cup pitted black olives, sliced
    1 tablespoon green onion, finely chopped

Combine cheeses and spread over pie crust. To eggs, add remaining ingredients and blend. Pour egg mixture over cheeses in pie crust. Bake at 350° for 45 minutes or until done (knife inserted will come out clean). If using a fresh pie crust, mix dough with 1 teaspoon chili powder and omit this ingredient from egg mixture.

EGG QUICHE
(serves 6)

    1/2 cup melted butter
    1 teaspoon baking powder
    1/2 cup flour
    10 eggs, slightly beaten
    3 4-ounce cans green chili, chopped
    1 pound monterey jack cheese, grated
    2 cups cottage cheese
    salt and pepper to taste

Blend together butter, baking powder, flour, and eggs. Add green chili, cheeses, salt, and pepper to egg mixture. Pour into a greased 9 x 12 inch pan. Bake at 400° for 15 minutes and then reduce heat to 350° for 35-45 minutes more.

HUEVOS RANCHEROS
(serves 6)

    1 cup green chili sauce or red salsa
    2 tablespoons butter
    6 eggs
    6 flour tortillas, warmed
    1 pound monterey jack cheese, grated

Heat sauce to boiling and remove from heat. In a large skillet, melt butter. Fry eggs over easy. Place one fried egg on each tortilla. Top with heated sauce and cheese.

EGGS WITH POTATOES
(serves 2)

    2 small potatoes, chopped
    1 tablespoon vegetable oil
    2 tablespoons onion, chopped
    1 tablespoon bell pepper, chopped
    1 tomato, chopped
    4 eggs, beaten
    1/8 teaspoon pepper
    1/2 teaspoon salt
    2 flour tortillas
    salsa (optional)

In a skillet, sauté potatoes in oil until tender. Add onion, bell pepper, and tomato and sauté until tender. Stir in beaten eggs, salt, and pepper. Scramble until set and serve with warm flour tortillas. May be topped with salsa, if desired.

GREEN CHILI AND EGGS
(serves 4-6)

    8 eggs
    1/2 onion, chopped
    1 4-ounce can green chili, chopped
    4 ounces longhorn cheddar cheese, grated
    1/8 teaspoon ground cumin
    1/8 teapoon onion powder
    1/2 teaspoon worcestershire sauce
    salt and pepper to taste
    3 tablespoons butter or margarine

Beat eggs. Add remaining ingredients except butter and stir well. Melt butter in skillet and stir in mixture. Scramble until set. Serve with warm flour tortillas.

VEGETABLES

SWEET NOODLE PUDDING
(serves 10-12)

    1 large package medium-broad noodles
    1 teaspoon cinnamon
    salt to taste (about 1/4 teaspoon)
    1 cup raisins
    1/2 cup sugar
    2 teaspoons almond extract
    2 cups milk
    3 eggs, beaten
    1/4 pound butter

Boil noodles according to package instructions. Drain and run under cold water to remove excess starch. To noodles, add cinnamon, salt, raisins, sugar, and almond extract. Combine milk and eggs and fold into noodles. Melt 1/2 of butter and add to mixture. Put the remaining butter in the baking casserole and heat. When butter is hot, pour in noodle mixture. Bake at 350° until pudding is golden brown.

SQUASH CASSEROLE
(serves 8)

    2 pounds squash (zucchini, yellow, etc.), sliced
    4 eggs
    1/2 cup milk
    1 pound longhorn cheddar cheese or monterey jack cheese, grated
    1/2 teaspoon salt
    2 teaspoons baking powder
    3 tablespoons flour
    1/4 cup parsley, chopped
    1 cup green chili, chopped
    1-1/2 cups crushed tortilla chips

SQUASH CASSEROLE (continued)

Cook squash in small amount of water until almost tender. Do not cook thoroughly! Drain and cool. Combine rest of ingredients except tortilla chips. Toss lightly with squash. Sprinkle bottom of lightly greased baking dish with tortilla chip crumbs. Pour in squash mixture and top with more crumbs. Bake at 350° for 30 minutes.

ZUCCHINI BOATS

    3 plump zucchini
    6 tablespoons butter
    1 clove garlic
    1/2 cup onion, chopped
    2 tomatoes, chopped
    1 4-ounce can green chili, chopped
    3/4 cup bread crumbs
    1/4 cup parmesan cheese
    salt and pepper to taste
    1 tablespoon parsley

Wash zucchini and cut in half lengthwise. Scoop out shells and reserve pulp. Sauté garlic and onion in 3 tablespoons butter until onion is transparent. Remove garlic clove. Add zucchini pulp, tomatoes, and chili to sautéed onions and mix well. Fill shells with mixture. Melt remaining butter and mix with bread crumbs, cheese, salt, pepper, and parsley. Heap each zucchini boat with bread crumb mixture. Cover and bake in buttered baking dish at 350° for 30 minutes.

CALABACITAS (ZUCCHINI CORN TREAT)
(serves 6)

    1/4 pound butter
    2 tablespoons onion, minced
    1 garlic clove

CALABACITAS (continued)

　　　3 zucchini, sliced
　　　1 4-ounce can green chili, chopped
　　　1 package frozen corn, thawed
　　　salt and pepper to taste

Sauté onion and garlic in butter until brown. Remove garlic. Add zucchini and sauté until almost soft - do not overcook! Add chili, thawed corn, salt, and pepper. Heat and serve.

LEMONED CARROTS
(serves 4-6)

　　　1 pound baby carrots
　　　2 tablespoons butter
　　　1 tablespoon lemon juice
　　　1/2 teaspoon garlic salt
　　　1/2 teaspoon dried basil, crushed
　　　dash of pepper

In a saucepan, cook carrots in boiling salted water for 20-25 minutes or until tender. Drain. In saucepan, melt butter. Stir in lemon juice, garlic salt, basil, and pepper. Add carrots and gently toss.

BROCCOLI-RICE CASSEROLE
(serves 4-6)

　　　1 cup rice
　　　2/3 cup onion, diced
　　　2/3 cup celery, diced
　　　2 tablespoons cooking oil
　　　1 package frozen chopped broccoli, thawed and drained
　　　1 can cream of mushroom soup
　　　2/3 cup milk
　　　1 8-ounce jar processed cheese spread
　　　1 cup green chili, chopped

BROCCOLI-RICE CASSEROLE (continued)

Cook rice according to package directions. Sauté onion and celery in oil. Add thawed broccoli. Simmer on low heat for 15 minutes. To broccoli, add soup, milk, cheese, and chili and blend well. Add cooked rice. Stir well and pour into greased baking dish. Bake 25 minutes at 350° until well heated.

QUELITES (SPINACH WITH BEANS)
(serves 6-8)

    2 10-ounce packages frozen spinach
    1 tablespoon bacon grease
    3 tablespoons onion, chopped
    1 garlic clove, minced
    1/4 teaspoon chili powder
    1 teaspoon salt
    2 cups pinto beans (see index or use canned beans)

Cook spinach as directed on package. Drain. Sauté onion and garlic in bacon grease until tender. Add spinach, chili powder, salt, and beans. Simmer 5 minutes.

PINTO BEANS

    1-pound package dried pinto beans
    1 large onion, chopped
    1 clove garlic
    3 slices bacon
    2 teaspoons chili powder
    1 10-ounce can tomatoes and green chili
    1 tablespoon salt

Wash beans thoroughly. Place in pot and cover with water. Soak overnight. In the morning, drain beans and discard any that look bad. Place

PINTO BEANS (continued)

beans in large cooking pot and add 4 cups of cold water. Bring to a boil. Reduce heat and add other ingredients except salt. Simmer 4 hours, adding hot water as it is needed to keep beans moist. After first 3 hours of cooking, add salt. Beans should be soft and the juice thick.

FRIJOLES REFRITOS (REFRIED BEANS)
(serves 4)

>   2 cups cooked pinto beans, mashed (see index or use 1 can frijoles refritos)
>   3 tablespoons bacon grease
>   1 cup longhorn cheese, grated

In a frying pan, add beans to melted bacon grease. Blend and heat well. Add cheese, again blending well. Serve hot. Top with more grated cheese, if desired.

EGGPLANT MEXICANO
(serves 6-8)

>   1 large eggplant
>   olive oil
>   1 pound canned tomatoes, chopped
>   1/2 cup green chili, chopped
>   2 tablespoons minced onion
>   1/2 teaspoon ground cumin
>   1/2 teaspoon garlic salt
>   1 cup cheddar cheese, grated
>   1/2 cup sour cream
>   sliced black olives (optional)

Wash and slice eggplant into 1/3-inch slices. Brush each side of each slice with olive oil and place on cookie sheet. Bake 20 minutes at 350° until fork tender. Combine tomatoes, chili, onion, cumin, and

EGGPLANT MEXICANO (continued)

garlic salt and simmer 10-20 minutes. In a greased casserole, layer eggplant, sauce, and cheese. Repeat layers. Top with cheese, sour cream, and olives if desired. Bake at 350° for 20 minutes or until bubbly.

CHILIES AND CORN
(serves 4)

>1 package frozen corn
>2 tablespoons vegetable oil
>1/4 cup green chili, chopped
>1 clove garlic, minced
>salt and pepper to taste
>pinch of sugar

Cook corn in water, just until thawed. Drain. Heat vegetable oil in frying pan and add all ingredients. Cover pan and cook slowly for 15 minutes. If mixture seems a little dry, add a few drops of water.

BAKED CORN PUDDING
(serves 4-6)

>2 eggs, beaten
>2 cups cream-style corn
>1 cup yellow cornmeal
>3/4 teaspoon garlic salt
>1/2 teaspoon baking powder
>1 cup butter, melted
>3/4 cup buttermilk
>2 medium onions, chopped
>2 cups sharp cheddar cheese, grated
>1 4-ounce can green chili, chopped and drained

BAKED CORN PUDDING (continued)

In a bowl, combine all ingredients except cheese and chili and mix well. Turn half the mixture into a greased baking dish and cover with half the cheese and all of the chili. Sprinkle remainder of cheese over chili and top with remaining corn mixture. Bake 1 hour at 350°.

MEXICAN GREEN BEANS
(serves 4)

    1 tablespoon vegetable oil
    1/4 cup onion, chopped
    1 clove garlic, minced
    1 large tomato, diced
    1/2 cup tomato juice
    1/4 teaspoon chili powder
    salt to taste
    1 package frozen green beans, thawed

Sauté onion and garlic in oil for 5 minutes. Add tomato, tomato juice, chili powder, and salt. When mixture comes to a boil, add green beans. Simmer covered 10-15 minutes.

RICE AND CHILI BAKE
(serves 6-8)

    1 cup rice
    2 cups sour cream
    1 cup green chili, chopped
    1 cup monterey jack cheese, cubed
    1 teaspoon salt

Cook rice according to package directions, undercooking slightly. Combine all ingredients and place in a greased casserole. Bake at 350° 15 minutes or until cheese melts and mixture is thoroughly heated.

INSTANT SPANISH RICE
(serves 4)

    1/4 cup onion, chopped
    1 clove garlic
    1 tablespoon vegetable oil
    2 large tomatoes, chopped
    1/4 teaspoon salt
    1/2 cup chicken broth
    1/2 teaspoon chili powder
    1/8 teaspoon ground cumin
    1 cup instant rice

Sauté onion and garlic in oil until tender. Add tomatoes, salt, chicken broth, chili powder, and cumin. Bring to a boil and stir in rice. Cover and simmer on very low heat 15-20 minutes or until liquid is absorbed.

SPANISH RICE DE MEXICO
(serves 4)

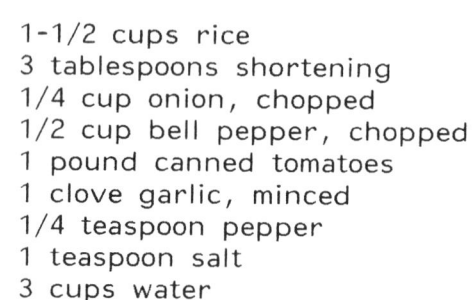

    1-1/2 cups rice
    3 tablespoons shortening
    1/4 cup onion, chopped
    1/2 cup bell pepper, chopped
    1 pound canned tomatoes
    1 clove garlic, minced
    1/4 teaspoon pepper
    1 teaspoon salt
    3 cups water

Brown rice in shortening until golden brown. Add onion, bell pepper, tomatoes, garlic, pepper, salt, and 1-1/2 cups water to cover. Cover and simmer slowly until rice mixture is almost dry. Add 1/2 cup cold water, a little at a time, cooking over low heat, until fluffy.

DESSERTS

BISCOCHITOS

    1 pound lard
    1 cup sugar
    1 teaspoon anise seed
    2 eggs
    6 cups flour, sifted
    1 teaspoon baking powder
    1 teaspoon salt
    1/4 cup water
    1/4 cup sugar
    1 tablespoon cinnamon

Cream lard thoroughly in electric mixer. Add sugar and anise seed. Beat eggs, add to lard mixture, and blend until light and fluffy. Sift flour with baking powder and salt and add to lard mixture. Add water and knead until well mixed. Roll to 1/2 inch thickness and cut into fancy shapes. Combine sugar and cinnamon and sprinkle onto tops of cookies. Bake at 350° until lightly browned, about 10 minutes.

LAS CRUCES PECAN PIE

    3 eggs, beaten
    1 cup sugar
    1 cup dark karo syrup
    1 teaspoon vanilla extract
    3 tablespoons melted butter (cooled)
    1 9-inch pie shell, frozen
    1-1/2 cups pecans

Slightly thaw pie shell. Combine eggs and sugar, mixing together slightly. Add karo syrup, vanilla, and melted butter to egg mixture. Fold into pie shell. Gently top with pecans. Preheat oven to.

LAS CRUCES PECAN PIE (continued)

350°. Place pie pan on cookie sheet and bake at 350° for 10 minutes. Reduce heat to 325° and bake for 40-45 minutes. Cool and serve.

CHRISTMAS FRUIT CAKE

    3 eggs, beaten
    1/2 cup cooking oil
    1/2 cup milk
    2-1/2 cups flour, sifted
    1 cup sugar
    1 teaspoon baking powder
    1 teaspoon baking soda
    1 teaspoon cinnamon
    1/2 teaspoon salt
    2 cups carrots, shredded
    1/4 cup flaked coconut
    1/2 cup fresh cranberries, chopped
    1/2 cup raisins
    1/2 cup chopped pecans

Grease and flour 2 loaf pans. Preheat oven to 375°. Reduce heat to 350° when placing loaf pans in oven. Combine eggs, oil, and milk. Combine flour, sugar, baking powder, baking soda, cinnamon, and salt in separate dish. Add egg mixture to dry ingredients. Stir in carrots, coconut, cranberries, raisins, and pecans. Turn into pans and fill to half-way mark. Bake 30-35 minutes. Cake is done when an inserted toothpick comes out clean.

RUM-FLAVORED BANANAS
(serves 6)

    1/3 cup butter
    1/2 cup brown sugar
    6 bananas, sliced lengthwise
    cinnamon

RUM-FLAVORED BANANAS (continued)

    1/4 cup rum
    1/2 cup whipping cream
    1/4 cup powdered sugar
    1/4 teaspoon vanilla extract

Melt butter and brown sugar in a large fry pan. Sprinkle bananas with cinnamon and sauté in butter/sugar mixture 1 minute on each side. Sprinkle in the rum. Combine whipping cream, powdered sugar, and vanilla. Top bananas with whipped cream mixture.

MEXICAN HONEY DAINTIES
(yields 2-1/2 to 3 dozen)

    1/3 cup cooking oil
    1/2 cup unsalted butter, softened
    1/3 cup sugar
    1 tablespoon orange juice
    1 teaspoon baking powder
    1/2 teaspoon baking soda
    1-3/4 to 2 cups all-purpose flour
    3/4 cup sugar
    1/2 cup water
    1/3 cup honey
    1/3 cup pecans, finely chopped

In mixer bowl, beat together cooking oil and butter until blended. Beat in the sugar. Add orange juice, baking powder, and baking soda. Mix well. Add enough of the flour, a little at a time, to make a medium-soft dough. Shape dough into 2-inch ovals and place on an ungreased baking sheet. Bake in 350° preheated oven for 20-25 minutes or until cookies are golden. Meanwhile, in a saucepan, combine sugar, water, and honey. Boil gently uncovered for 5 minutes. Cool. Dip face of cookies into warm syrup and then press into chopped nuts. Let dry. Store in covered container or freeze for later use.

PECAN COOKIES
(yields 3-1/2 to 4 dozen)

    1 cup unsalted butter
    1/2 cup powdered sugar, sifted
    1 egg yolk
    2 tablespoons brandy
    1/2 teaspoon vanilla
    1/3 cup pecans, finely chopped
    2-1/4 cups all-purpose flour
    1/2 teaspoon baking powder
    sifted powdered sugar

In mixer bowl, cream together butter and powdered sugar. Add the egg yolk, brandy, and vanilla; mix well. Stir in the pecans. Stir together the flour and baking powder and blend into the sugar mixture. Wrap and chill the dough about 30 minutes. Form dough into 1-inch balls or ovals. Place on an ungreased baking sheet. Bake in a 325° oven 20-25 minutes or until cookies are a light sand color. Cool and roll in additional powdered sugar.

EMPANADITAS DE FRUTA
(yields 6-9 dozen)

Filling

    1 pound dried apples, peaches, or apricots
    water
    2-1/2 cups sugar
    1/2 teaspoon salt
    2 teaspoons cinnamon
    1 teaspoon nutmeg
    1 cup raisins, soaked in warm water

Simmer fruit in small amount of water until soft and mushy. Add small amount of water as needed. Drain. Mash fruit and add remaining ingredients, mixing well. Cool and fill dough rounds, cooking as directed.

EMPANADITAS DE FRUTA (continued)

Dough

1 teaspoon active dry yeast
1-1/2 cups warm water
1/4 cup lard or shortening
4 cups flour
1 teaspoon salt
1 tablespoon powdered sugar (optional)

Dissolve yeast in warm water. Set aside. Combine dry ingredients except sugar; cut in lard. Add yeast mixture and knead dough until smooth and elastic. Do not let rise. Roll dough out on floured surface to 1/4 or 1/8 inch thickness. Cut into rounds to desired size. Place small mound of filling in center of pastry and fold over, moistening edges and sealing well. Fry in deep hot vegetable oil until golden brown. Drain. Sprinkle with powdered sugar if desired.

NATILLAS
(serves 4)

2 eggs, separated
3/4 cup sugar
2 tablespoons flour
1/8 teaspoon salt
2 cups milk
nutmeg or cinnamon

Beat egg yolks and stir in sugar, flour, and salt. Cream until smooth. To saucepan, add milk and stir in yolk mixture. Cook over medium heat, stirring constantly until mixture boils and thickens. Remove from heat. Beat egg whites until stiff and fold into milk mixture. Sprinkle with nutmeg or cinnamon and chill before serving in individual dishes.

CAPIROTADA (BREAD PUDDING)

10 slices of bread
3 cups water
1/2 cup sugar
1 teaspoon cinnamon
1/2 teaspoon nutmeg
1/2 teaspoon cloves, ground
1/4 teaspoon salt
1 cup cheddar cheese, grated
1 cup raisins
2 tablespoons butter
1/2 cup red wine

Toast bread and break into 2-inch pieces. In saucepan, combine water, sugar, spices, and salt. Bring to a boil and simmer for 10 minutes. Grease a 2-quart baking dish. Layer bread, cheese, raisins, butter, and wine. Pour syrup over pudding and bake at 350° for 15 minutes or until all syrup is dissolved. Serve warm or cold.

FLAN

1/2 cup sugar
1 quart milk
1/2 cup sugar
1 teaspoon vanilla
2-inch cinnamon stick (optional)
pinch of salt
4 eggs
6 egg yolks

In heavy saucepan, cook 1/2 cup sugar over medium heat until sugar melts, stirring constantly. Continue stirring and cooking, adjusting heat as necessary to prevent burning until sugar is caramelized and golden brown. Quickly pour into a mold and tip from side to side to coat bottom and half way up sides evenly. Set aside to cool.

FLAN (continued)

In saucepan, heat milk. Add sugar, vanilla, salt, and cinnamon, if desired. Simmer for 15 minutes. Set aside to cool. Beat eggs and egg yolks together. Add them to cooled milk and stir well. Pour mixture through strainer into the caramel-covered mold. Cover the mold and set in a hot water bath, half way up side of mold, on bottom shelf of oven. Cook at 350° for 1 to 2 hours, until knife inserted in center comes out clean. Cool and refrigerate. When ready to serve (flan should be made one day in advance of serving), cover mold with large platter. Invert mold onto platter. Remove mold. Caramel will be a liquid sauce. Before inverting mold, tip to be sure flan slithers and caramel is not hardened which will happen if it is cooked too much. Do not attempt to unmold if caramel is solid. Place mold in warm water and test again. Do not loosen with knife. Repeat warm water method again until loose.

SHERBET SURPRISE
(serves 8)

  3 cups sugar
  6 cups water
  1 teaspoon lime peel, grated
  1 cup lime juice
  1/2 cup tequila
  2 egg whites
  1/4 teaspoon salt

Bring sugar and water to a boil. Add lime peel. When syrupy, remove from heat and stir in lime juice. Freeze until thick. Place mixture in blender; add tequila, egg white, and salt. Blend thoroughly. Refreeze until ready to serve. Whirl in blender to soften, if desired.

INDEX

APPETIZERS

	Page
Albondigas	12
Albuquerque Delight	7
Biscuit Pizza	19
Broccoli Dip	7
Cheese Crisp	15
Cheese Crisp with Guacamole	15
Cheese Quiche	16
Chili-Cheese Balls	14
Chili-Cheese Log	14
Chili-Cheese Sticks	18
Chili con Queso	8
Chili Egg Rolls	11
Chili-Pecan Balls	14
Chili Pie	16
Chili-Stuffed Mushrooms	18
Chili Tempura	10
Chili Won Tons	11
Easy Chili con Queso	8
Empañadas	64
Fondue Mexicana	13
Green Chili Dip	8
Green Chili Salsa	6
Guacamole	10
Hot Carne Adovada Canapes	19
Jalapeño Bean Dip	9
Nachos	17
Picadillo Almond Dip	9
Picante Sauce	5
Quesadillas	17
Sour Cream-Chili Dip	10
Spicy Cashews	13
Taco Sauce with Jalapeños	6
Taquitas	39
Tortilla Chips	5
Tossed Shrimp	12

BEVERAGES

Bebido de Strawberry	21
Café Kahlúa	20
Café Mexicana	21
New Mexican Hot Chocolate	22
Margaritas	22
Spanish Coffee	21
Spiced Tea	20

BREADS

Buñuelos	25
Indian Fry Bread	25
Mexican Spoon Bread	27
Molletes	26
Sopaipillas	24
Corn Tortillas	23
Flour Tortillas	23

DESSERTS

	Page
Biscochitos (anise cookies)	81
Capirotada (bread pudding)	86
Christmas Fruitcake	82
Empanaditas de Fruta	84
Flan	86
Las Cruces Pecan Pie	81
Mexican Honey Dainties	83
Natillas	85
Pecan Cookies	84
Rum-Flavored Bananas	82
Sherbet Surprise	87

EGG DISHES

Cheese Quiche	70
Chili and Mushroom Omelet	68
Chorizo and Eggs	68
Egg Quiche	70
Eggs with Potatoes	71
Green Chili and Eggs	72
Huevos Rancheros	71
Spanish Omelet	69

MAIN DISHES

Albondigas	12
All-in-One Casserole	60
Arroz con Pollo	55
Authentic Cheese Enchiladas	45
Baked Chicken Enchilada Casserole	47
Baked Chilies Rellenos	49
Barbecue Shrimp	54
Beef Enchilada Casserole	48
Burritos	65
Carne Adovada	40
Carne Asada	63
Chalupas	52
Chicken and Green Chili	58
Chicken and Rice Casserole	58
Chicken Burritos	66
Chicken Enchiladas	46
Chili-Chicken Roll Ups	59
Chili con Carne Americano	43
Chili con Carne de Albuquerque	43
Chili con Carne Rojo	44
Chilies Rellenos	49
Chimichangas	66
Chorizo	36
Easy Enchilada Casserole	47
Easy Meatless Casserole	52
Eggplant Casserole	50
Empañadas	64

	Page
MAIN DISHES	
Enchiladas - Red or Green	46
Fajitas	67
Garlic-Flavored Sole	55
Green Chili-Cheese Bake	51
Green Chili-Chicken Divan	56
Green Chili Stew	36
Green Chili Stroganoff	62
Guacamole-Tomato Salad	51
Mexican Chicken	57
Oven Fried Chicken	57
Pork and Red Chili	61
Pork Burritos	65
Pork Chili con Carne	45
Posole	37
Shrimp Olé	53
Shrimp Salad	54
Sour Cream Enchiladas	46
Spinach and Beef Casserole	61
Steak Roll Ups	62
Tacos	38
Taco Salad	40
Tamales	41
Taquitas	39
Texas Tacos	39
Turkey-Tortilla Casserole	59

PREPARATION, TECHNIQUES AND SAUCES	
Blender Green Chili Sauce	2
Chili	1
Green Chili Salsa	6
Green Chili Sauce	2
Preparation of Dried Red Chilies	3
Preparation of Fresh Green Chili	1
Preparation of Fresh Red Chili	4
Red Chili Powder	3
Taco Sauce with Jalapeños	6

SALADS	
Cauliflower Salad	34
Eggplant Salad	35
Guacamole	10
Macaroni and Cheese Salad	34
Southwestern Potato Salad	35
Tossed Shrimp	12

	Page
SOUPS	
Avocado Soup	28
Chicken and Cabbage Soup	33
Chili Chicken Soup	33
Cream of Zucchini Soup	28
Gazpacho	31
Mexican Meatball Soup	30
Mexican Vegetable Soup	29
Pinto Bean Soup	30
Racey Lacey Tomato Soup	29
Tortilla Chicken Soup	32
Zesty Cheese Soup	31
Zucchini Soup	27

VEGETABLES	
Baked Corn Pudding	78
Broccoli-Rice Casserole	75
Calabacitas (zucchini corn treat)	74
Chilies and Corn	78
Eggplant Mexicano	77
Frijoles Refritos (refried beans)	77
Instant Spanish Rice	80
Lemoned Carrots	75
Mexican Green Beans	79
Pinto Beans	76
Quelites	76
Rice and Chili Bake	79
Spanish Rice de Mexico	80
Squash Casserole	73
Sweet Noodle Pudding	73
Zucchini Boats	74

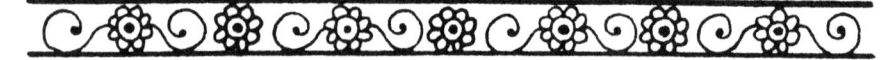

For additional copies of FIESTA MEXICANA, send $7.95 **to:**

    T & E Enterprises
    P. O. Box 14324
    Albuquerque, New Mexico 87191

Allow 4-6 weeks for delivery.